HISTORICAL ROOTS OF INDUSTRIAL ENTREPRENEURSHIP IN INDIA AND JAPAN

Historical Roots of Industrial Entrepreneurship in India and Japan

A Comparative Interpretation

DWIJENDRA TRIPATHI

MANOHAR
2026

First published 1997
Reprinted 2025, 2026

ISBN 978-81-7304-196-9

Published by
Ajay Kumar Jain for
Manohar Publishers & Distributors
4753/23 Ansari Road, Daryaganj
New Delhi 110 002

Printed and bound in India

TO
KUSUM SHRIVASTAVA
IN PARTIAL REPAYMENT
OF A BAD DEBT

Contents

Preface

CONTRARY TO the popular belief, the fountainhead of all historical research is the present. For, the questions that the historian seeks to answer arise out of the concerns of his times and surroundings. True, he explores the past for his answers, but his relations with the past is like a scientist's relations with his laboratory. The historian is not concerned with the past any more than the scientist is with his laboratory. This is perhaps what Frederick Jackson Turner had in mind when he said that every generation writes its own history.

All my work in Indian business history has been informed by this basic approach. My purpose has been to comprehend the essential dynamics of Indian business behaviour and correct many popular misconceptions about it. This work is a part of this effort. By placing its experience alongside that of another country, with which it is frequently compared. I hope to provide a more balanced explanation for India's inability to register a faster pace of industrial progress.

This study is not a comprehensive business history of either of the countries under focus. It is limited to analysing the differential scenario in respect of emergence, perception and exploitation of industrial opportunities during the formative periods of industrialization in the two countries. This has been done using the data available in a large number of secondary but authentic works, and arranging them against a conceptual framework developed on the basis of my previous researches. It is thus more in the nature of an interpretative work than one based on basic research. However, only such information has been utilized on which a broad consensus has already emerged.

I completed most of my research for this study during a year's stay in Japan on a fellowship offered by the Institute of Developing Economies (IDE), Tokyo a few years ago. The Indian Institute of Management, Ahmedabad, my employers in India then, granted me leave of absence to avail myself of the opportunity. My debt of gratitude to these institutions is great indeed. Another organization which should be mentioned is the library of the Department of Economics, the University of Tokyo, which granted me free access to its rich collections.

The number of persons who helped me in a variety of ways is too large to permit individual acknowledgement. A few, however, stand out. Shigemochi Hirashima went much beyond his responsibilities as the Director of International Exchange Department at the IDE when he allowed me to draw freely on his insights and understanding of the Japanese as well as Indian situations. Shoji Ito during the entire course of my research remained an academic counsellor and guide. Others at the IDE who helped in clarifying some crucial aspects of my research include Hiroichi Yamaguchi, Minoru Ouchi, Hiroshi Sato and Fumiko Oshikawa. Shusaku Matsumoto and his associates in the IDE library helped in identifying and locating indispensable reference materials. The administrative staff of the International Exchange Department, particularly Tadashi Ishida, Takao Tsuneishi, and Kyoko Fujisawa took care of all the logistic facilities without which no serious research would have been possible. Leoncio D. Miralao, Jr. Radha Sinha, and Momtaz Ahmed among the fellow visiting researchers provided a sounding board, as it were, to check and cross-check my ideas and hypotheses.

Some persons out of the IDE-fold also helped me in clarifying my thinking. Prominent among those are Keichiro Nakagawa, Shinichi Yonekawa, Hiroshi Kitamura, Masami Kita, Yoko Sano, Sho Sekiya, A. Mikami, Hiroshi Fukazawa, Toru Matsui, Masanori Koga, Hisashi Nakamura, Yukihiko Kiyokawa and Jözen Takeuchi. Y. Mutaguchi and his gracious wife not only provided me shelter but also made me feel at home in a far off and relatively unfamiliar land.

Purnima Upadhyay helped compile the bibliography, and Pramod A. Shah typed the script.

While I will continue to be grateful to all these persons for their generosity and consideration, the responsibility for any error, omission, or misrepresentation must, of course, remain mine.

Ahmedabad DWIJENDRA TRIPATHI
4 April 1997

CHAPTER I

Introduction

COMPARATIVE STUDIES in entrepreneurship are few and far between. Even fewer have been the attempts to compare historically the experiences and processes of entrepreneurial developments in various societies. Perhaps because entrepreneurship is a relatively new area of enquiry, scholars have been more concerned with the scenario in individual countries in this sphere rather than attempting cross-national analysis.[1] Also, most of the existing works have their focus on the present, instead of on a long time horizon. While the usefulness of such works for understanding the entrepreneurial phenomenon is undeniable (for the inductive process is the only meaningful route to a general comprehension), cross-national comparisons undoubtedly will yield a much deeper insight and provide a more secure base for generalisation. Now that the literature on entrepreneurial endeavours in various countries is not very meagre, it is perhaps time to turn our attention to comparative study. This is what this work intends to do.

Our focus on the industrial aspect needs no explanation. After all, this has been traditionally the most visible manifestation of creative economic urges in a society. However, the reasons for choosing Japan and India for our purpose may not be as obvious. It may be argued, for instance, that as Japan and India today stand at two extremes of the industrial horizon, comparison between them would be meaningless. The argument, however, misses the fact that modern industries made their debut in both these countries almost simultaneously—in fact a little earlier in India which was 'the first of the oriental countries to feel [the] impact of industrialization'.[2] The country already had about 10 cotton mills before the Meiji Restoration paved the ground for the rise of factory production in Japan. But while industrialization proceeded at a very rapid pace in Japan to place that country in the category of highly advanced nations within a relatively short period, factory industry in India grew at a snail's pace, leaving it far behind its competitor of yore. As the speed of the one and the slovenliness of the other in the race for industrial progress have something to do with the respective entrepreneurial urges and manifestations of these two peoples, a comparative enquiry into the factors influencing their motivation and performance in this crucial area would provide valuable input for understanding the entrepreneurial phenomenon.

We seek to review the experiences of these two countries historically because scanning and analysing the present alone often leads to a partial and lopsided view of the forces impinging on the entrepreneurial behaviour of a people. History, providing a long-term view of things, helps us appreciate the process of change along with continuity, distinguish the intrinsic elements in a people's responses to events and things from the extrinsic and integrate them to obtain a comprehensive pattern of their behaviour. No comparison can be meaningful without a long-term perspective.

Some explanations, of course have been offered for the differential performance of Japan and India on the industrial front. The most pervasive and widely accepted of these is that while the Indian initiative had to reckon with the debilitating effect of colonialism, the early promoters of factory production in Japan benefited from the nurturing care of state patronage and support. As one of the proponents of this view, after surveying Japan's industrial growth between 1880 and 1940, put it:

> As a result of various State policies and the initiative, enterprise and skill of the Japanese farmer, small industrialists and big entrepreneurs, Japan experienced a rate of growth . . . which was equalled only by Sweden and post-1929 Russia . . . . Japan's example shows what could have been done in India. . . . However, the Indian government had objectives other than economic development.[3]

Most works analysing the Indian economic scene during the British rule echo this view in some way or the other. So deeply entrenched is the argument centered around colonial exploitation that attempts to shake it up through some well-reasoned correctives have had little impact.[4]

According to another view, shared by the scholars of differing ideological persuasions, India's failure to develop its industrial structure fast enough was due to the restrictive role of its religious-cultural values and social organization which generated an uneconomic outlook among its people.[5] Direct comparison with

Japan has been less frequent in this respect, but at least one scholar has found the secret of differential development in the two oriental societies in the character and quality of native entrepreneurs.[6] Also, it will be difficult to find many works which do not attribute economic change in that Pacific country to its social organization and cultural ethos or to the Japanese way of doing things. It is fairly common these days to explain the recent spectacular economic performance of Japan with reference to *nihonjin-ron*—a term which has been so variously interpreted that to find an exact English equivalent is not easy, but it can be roughly translated as 'cultural roots of Japanese behaviour pattern'.[7]

A third explanation has been offered by those who do not accept either of the above formulations. They seem to suggest that the secret of differential economic performance of the two countries may lie in their contrasting physical dimensions—one being so large and the other so small in comparison.[8] This argument, however, is too simplistic to detain us. That a number of large countries, some of continental proportions, have experienced impressive economic growth and many of much smaller sizes have remained backward would be sufficient to expose its weakness. Seen in a proper perspective, the other two explanations appear to be only slightly more convincing, but not sufficiently so.

Let us first deal with what may be called the political argument. It cannot be sustained unless we believe that the role of the state is the *only* critical factor in the economic rejuvenation of a people. Simply because Japan and India both set off on the industrial course almost simultaneously does not necessarily mean that both started off with equal advantages, or the basic conditions necessary for industrial rejuvenation were similar in both these countries in every respect except the nature of the state. And if this was not so, the differential progress in the two countries cannot be attributed only to the differences in the level and quality of state encouragement to industrialization. The pace of progress in a country starting, on balance, from a more favourable position is bound to be quicker than in its less advantageously placed counterpart; variation with respect to one single factor, like the level and quality of state support to industrial change, may cause only marginal difference. For, a structure rising on a relatively narrow or slender base would develop much more cautiously and therefore much more slowly.[9]

To argue that the state in colonial India was far less enthusiastic about, if not downright hostile towards, the promotion industrialization than in Meiji Japan is to stress a truism. No colonial power can be accused of the sinful act of wilfully inducing industrial change in a subject country, and certainly not at a time when the doctrine of *laissez faire* was ruling the roost. But the policies and programmes pursued by a government, colonial or otherwise, seldom proceed on their projected course, and their total impact on the entrepreneurial climate, vision and manifestation in the society in question is not always what may be intended by such policies and programmes. The by-products flowing indirectly, and in many cases unintendedly from these policies and programmes may have as much, if not more, significance for a proper understanding of the dynamics of entrepreneurship in the society concerned. The political argument pays no or less than sufficient attention to the forces set in motion unintentionally by the British imperial presence, which brought about a qualitative change in the Indian climate for enterprise, and harps almost exclusively on the paralysing effect of colonialism. In the same vein, it seems to unduly overstress the role of the state in generating a more wholesome entrepreneurial climate in Japan, and underestimate the contribution of the preconditions which had already developed before the Meiji Restoration. Without intending to do so, the proponents of this argument would have us believe that it is the role of the state that determines, to the exclusion of all other factors, the course of entrepreneurship development in a country—a position that can be sustained neither theoretically nor empirically.

The socio-cultural explanation is even less persuasive. First, it seems to proceed from the assumption that culture precedes history. The fact of the matter is that culture evolves as history proceeds; it is history's companion and not its determinant. Or history determines the course of culture as much as culture determines the course of history; it is not a one-way process. To quote a well-known anthropologist:

> Each moment of history gives new alignments and relationships, new interactions and oppositions. As people build their current culture out of the pieces of the old and live out their material conditions in new ways, so their social world takes on new configurations. The figurations give the

appearance of stability and timelessness, but they are only momentary as people realign and force movement. The forces prompting realignments come from people learning and choosing and, perhaps more often, struggling to learn and choose over time.[10]

Socio-cultural values, thus, cannot be percieved as remaining immune to or insulated against pressure from changes in material conditions, as this explanation would have us believe. The conception that culture is something organismic or static runs counter to the entire human experience.

Secondly, it is by no means easy to identify with any degree of precision the value system of a society—much less so in cases of such complex societies as Japan and India. But even if we surmount this difficulty by identifying the value system of a people with their religious ethos and ideals, as the proponents of the socio-cultural school imply, our difficulties do not end. For, in neither case would it be possible to identify a single source of values. Was it Shintoism or Buddhism or Confucianism in Japan? To say that all these sources reinforced one another is to overlook a long history of conflict between the two major religious orders which flourished in Japan. And Confucianism, at any rate, was not a religion but a code of conduct which, if contrary to the religious ethos, could not have moulded the socio-economic behaviour. The Indian scene is even more complicated. To suggest, as has been done by the supporters of this line of reasoning, that the so-called Hindu value system was a major factor in shaping the Indian attitude to economic activities is to betray a fatal misunderstanding of the basic character of Hinduism. If by religion we mean an integrated system of beliefs and principles about man's relationship with the cosmos, Hinduism is far from being so. It essentially is a collectivity of sects and sub-sects, embracing myriad beliefs and principles—sometimes contradictory, sometimes complementary. Thus, neither Hinduism, nor the so-called Hindu value system can be an appropriate frame of reference for a meaningful analysis.

Thirdly, it cannot be maintained that the value system of Japan, emanating from its religious-cultural ethos, could have been more conducive to economic achievement than the value system engendered by Hinduism. For, neither Shintoism nor Buddhism in essence is any less spiritualistic and other-worldly than Hinduism is alleged to be. And the Hindu stress on material well-being (*artha* and *kama*) is in no way less pronounced than the Shinto/Buddhist emphasis on mundane, earthly matters. In the abstract theoretical sense then, there is nothing in the Japanese values which would have produced a more achievement-oriented personality than the Indian values. And to suggest, as the supporters of this view have done, that the Hindu value system was so powerful and pervasive that it had a significant impact on the economic behaviour of even the non-Hindus[11] whose share in the total population of India has in no way been inconsiderable, is to shut one's eyes to the considerable variations in the business exploits of non-Hindu communities such as Parsees and Muslims.

Yet another weakness of the cultural explanation is that it presupposes that the code of conduct prescribed by their respective religious systems—and this is what the religious cultural values represent—were in fact internalized by the people of these countries, and that their conduct in actual life conformed to what was purported to be the ideal. Never in the entire history of mankind has any society lived up to the prescribed moral injunctions. The Indian and Japanese people cannot be credited to have accomplished the impossible.

What has been said above about the religious-cultural values applies equally to social organization. For, the fourfold division of the society which characterized pre-industrial Japan—samurai, peasant, artisan, and merchant—was in many ways similar to the four-fold *varnashrama* scheme which had a tight grip on Indian society—Hindu society at any rate—before the process of modernization began. Backed by religious-cultural sanctions in conjunction with static material environment the social systems in both the countries remained a formidable bulwark against occupational mobility and freedom of economic choices, preventing for a long time a large number of talented persons from embracing business careers on account of the sheer accident of birth. This does not, however, mean that there was something inherently static in the social organizations of these societies and that the traditional structure was basically unamenable to change. Japan's success in adapting its social system to the forces of modernization after the Meiji Restoration is an eloquent testimony against such a view. If India was much slower in this respect, it does not mean that the Indian system was uniquely inflexible or organically less resilient. What it means is, as we shall see later, that the time-honoured social divisions in India had to reckon with a different set of forces.

We may also recall in this context that when the theory linking economic performance with socio-economic paradigm was postulated, all those countries that had achieved some degree of industrial transition belonged to the West. The Western experience naturally formed the basic input for this formulation, and the cultural values and social structure commonly associated with the West came to be regarded as essential preconditions for economic aggrandizement—individuality, competitiveness, acquisitiveness, maximization of wants, etc. In contrast, the features commonly associated with oriental societies such as India and Japan and their people—group orientation, regard for social hierarchy, concern for tradition and convention, consensual approach and so on—were regarded as inhibitive of economic aspiration and achievement, and therefore impediments to economic transformation of the society. In the absence of inputs to the contrary, the theory won for itself such widespread acceptance that even the Meiji era performance of Japan could not provide a sufficiently strong corrective, and oriental values and social systems continued to be looked down upon as antithetical to economic change not only by the Western scholars alone but also by the oriental observers themselves.[12] It is only after the spectacular industrial resurgence of Japan in recent years that it is being realised that every culture discovers its own dynamics of development.

To appreciate this dynamics, it is necessary to take into account the totality of influences operating on economic choices and accomplishments in a society, and it is the failure on this score that renders the two sets of explanations mentioned earlier unsatisfactory. While the anti-colonial school has placed preponderant emphasis on the role of the state to the virtual exclusion of other relevant forces in determining the course of entrepreneurial behaviour in these countries, the socio-cultural school has paid little heed to the impact of environmental changes on the socio-cultural ethos and consequent reorientation of attitude towards economic exertions. In other words, both sets of explanations are basically unifactoral in character while entrepreneurial response is a multifactoral phenomenon.

II

The multifactoral nature of entrepreneurial process needs some elucidation before we proceed with the substantive part of our analysis. This is necessary because there is a great deal of conceptual confusion about entrepreneur and entrepreneurship.

The confusion is partly due to the growing popular interest in the entrepreneurial phenomenon witnessed during the post-Second World War period. Almost until the onset of the 1950s, the terms 'entrepreneur' and 'entrepreneurship' remained confined to the exclusive domains of the economic theories, directed to disentangling the sources of profit accruing from a business enterprise. As the concern for economic development became all-pervasive and the role of the human factor in the development process gained wide recognition, the terms lost the unambiguous technical connotation the economic theorists had invested them with, and assumed a more generic meaning.

It is not uncommon these days to hear expressions like academic entrepreneur, political entrepreneur, social entrepreneur, and so on. Even those who professedly are more loyal to the original sense do not understand the same thing by these terms. For some, entrepreneurship denotes an economic endeavour, requiring imagination, drive, and creativity, but for a large number of persons it is simply synonymous with self-employment, regardless of the nature of activity. Borrowing a phrase that the late G.D.H. Cole long ago used for socialism one can say that entrepreneurship as a concept has, like a hat, lost its shape because everybody uses it—and does so to suit his own peculiar fashion.

This is not the place to resolve this confusion in any comprehensive manner.[13] For our limited purpose of evolving an analytical framework, we can accept as a starting point the precepts of some of the old, acknowledged masters, right from the classical school down to our own times. If we integrate their formulations disregarding the recent populist notions, we may agree with Arthur H. Cole that entrepreneurship consists in 'purposeful activity or integrated sequence of decisions of an individual or a group of individuals undertaken to initiate, organize, or aggrandize a profit-oriented business unit for the production or distribution of economic goods or services'.[14] The definition incorporates on one hand 'judgement, perseverance, knowledge of the world as well as of business', ability to bear risk, and take decisions under uncertainty—the basic attributes of an entrepreneur according to the older scholars[15]—and, on the other, 'innovation' or 'creative response' which for Schumpeter and other authorities closer to our own times are the essential hallmarks of entrepreneurship. And contrary to the popular notion, by innovation Schumpeter did not mean simply the development of a new method of production; it may also comprise a new product, the opening of a new market, the acquisition of a new source of raw materials, or the carrying out of a new organization of industry.[16]

There is a general consensus that conceptually the entrepreneurship process can be divided into three stages: (i) perception of new opportunities for profit; (ii) marshalling of resources and creation of a viable organization to exploit the perceived opportunities; and (iii) responsiveness to changes in perceivable opportunities. Possibility of innovation exists at every stage. But what makes for the perception of an opportunity; what beckons to the innovative path? The question was not relevant for the economic theorists, but the psychologists, who entered the field of entrepreneurial theory only recently, have found what they call achievement motivation to be the critical trajectory of entrepreneurial upsurge.[17] This, however, is begging the question. For, if the achievement motivation is not inborn, which these theorists concede, we still are left with the problem of determining the factors which create or at least sustain such an attitude. And why should the achievement motivation be manifested in business success alone? Or why should a high achiever choose only the economic sphere to express himself?

The fact of the matter is that entrepreneurship occurs when the personal attributes of an individual or a group of individuals are reinforced and sustained by the general environment in which he has to operate. Long before the psychologists made their appearance in the realm of entrepreneurial theory, the German tradition had laid special emphasis on the 'deeper insight into the social context of the enterprise' and Cole called attention to 'diverse psychological imperatives . . . and changing environmental forces'[18] as the twin factors influencing entrepreneurial decisions. In other words, entrepreneurship is the response of an individual or a group of individuals to the surrounding world. The individual and the environment, thus, must be considered as the two crucial elements in an integrated framework to explain entrepreneurial behaviour.

It must be stressed, however, that environment encompasses much more than merely socio-cultural values or the economic stimuli. It signifies a conglomerate of material conditions prevailing in a society at a given point of time. These include, in broad terms, political situation, economic infrastructure, social overheads, technological development, and commonly shared values, goals and ethos of a society. These factors, individually and collectively, should have similar impact on all members of the society at a given point of time. But it is seldom the case. It is common knowledge that in the same set of material conditions and cultural milieu some people discover a hidden opportunity, some others see a threat, and the majority remains unconcerned. This is because the appreciation of the environment on the part of an individual is, to a large extent, determined by his personal values which in turn are conditioned by factors specific to him, viz., his family affiliation and upbringing; the nature and level of his education and training, formal as well as informal; his contact and social reference group; the demonstration effect of the activities of others in or out of his own society; and a host of other such influences. This process of interaction between the general environment and the individual-specific factors produces an amalgam of forces which directs his occupational vision and choices on one hand and his approaches to strategies and structures on the other.

For the sake of conceptual brevity, and to distinguish it from what is generally meant by the trem environment, we would call this amalgam 'constellation of forces'. Representing a fusion of the ideational and the material, it is analogous to a chemical compound whose distinctive property is entirely different from the separate properties of its constituent elements, and every time the proportions of the constituents change, a new compound would emerge. Each entrepreneurial experience—or what we have called 'entrepreneurial initiative' in the following schematic framework—originates in the constellation of forces peculiar to it. Attempt to comprehend it through the application of a general formula as both the socio-cultural and the politico-economic schools have sought to do, is bound to lead to misleading results. Likewise, the pace, momentum, and magnitude of the exploits which an entrepreneurial initiative may lead to subsequently—we may call it 'entrepreneurial continuum' for the sake of brevity—must also be explained in the context of changes in the constellation of forces specific to the enterprise and its promoters.

This *schema* has several merits. First, it calls for separate analsysis of each entrepreneurial experience with a view to acquiring a proper understanding of its antecedents and growth. It can, thus, provide a meaningful appreciation of the forces behind differential responses to economic choices. In this sense, it is explanatory in character. Secondly, the *schema* is multifactoral rather than unifactoral. The concept of the constellation of forces is sufficiently elastic to accommodate all relevant influences, and their interplay with one another, that may determine the fate and course of an economic project. In this sense, it is open-ended. Thirdly, it eschews stereotyped, predetermined and *a priori* explanation of entrepreneurial manifestations. In this sense it is scientific. The greatest advantage of this approach, however, is that it can be used to analyse the process of entrepreneurship in any culture or society. It is, therefore, ideally suited for the study of comparative entrepreneurship.

We can now sum up our conceptual position thus: The study of entrepreneurship is the study of entrepreneurial initiatives and entrepreneurial continua informed by the constellation of forces impinging on the birth and expansion of productive business enterprises in space and time. In the light of this formulation, the distinction very often made between 'creative' or 'primary' and 'adaptive' or 'secondary' entrepreneurship does not appear to be very meaningful.[19] The distinguishing features of the two kinds of entrepreneurship have never been explicitly stated, but what the champions of this dichotomy seem to imply is that the society which may be the first or among the first to develop, and apply for business aggrandizement, a new production or managerial device is to be credited with the entrepreneurship of primary variety whereas the later adoptions of the same instrumentality with or without modification by other societies signify secondary entrepreneurship.

If, however, entrepreneurial experiences of various societies are to be assessed in the context of their respective constellations of forces, there would appear to be no qualitative difference between the first-stage development and later adaptation of a production

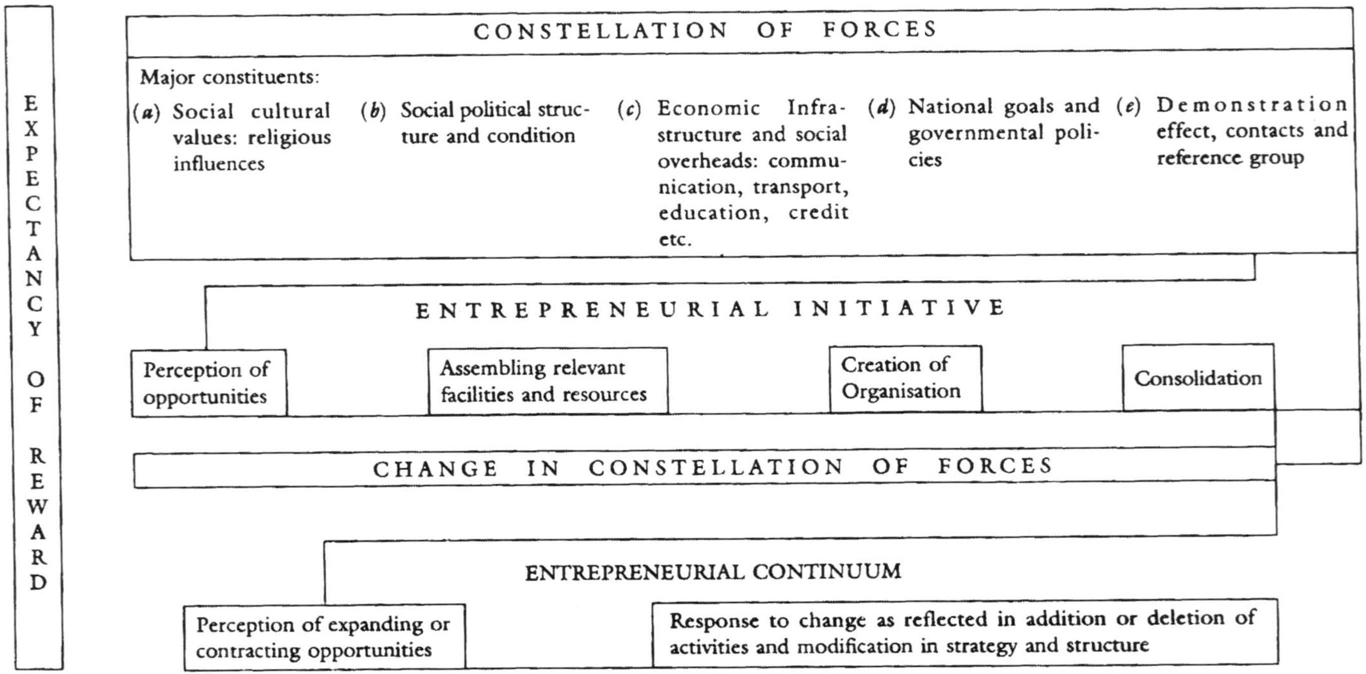

Note: Indicates that there is no automatic transition from one stage to the other. Casualty can occur at any stage.

FIG. 1: ENTREPRENEURIAL PROCESS

function. Both kinds of processes would involve similar risks if we make allowance for the variations in the risk-bearing capacities of the societies concerned. In embracing the technological processes initially developed in the West, the early entrepreneurs of colonial societies such as India, or other latecomers like Japan, displayed similar courage and exposed themselves to similar hazards as the entrepreneurs of Western countries experienced in perfecting these devices in the first instance.

All entrepreneurial acts, however, may not be equal in magnitude or impact. The activities of the nineteenth century railroad builders in the United States, for instance, important though they undoubtedly were, cannot be equated with Henry Ford's dazzling accomplishment in putting a whole society on the wheels. It is, therefore, useful to conceive of a hierarchy or gradation of entrepreneurship. However, to assign to a creative business experience its proper place in the entrepreneurial hierarchy is by no means easy. Neither the quantum of investment nor the volume of quantifiable profit can be a satisfactory guide, because if the investment does not result in a viable going concern, it would reflect badly on the entrepreneur's judgement. And empirical evidences can be multiplied to support the view that for an entrepreneur, return on investment comprises much more than mere monetary benefits.

The fact is that non-monetary, intangible benefit is as important a constituent of the expectancy of reward from an entrepreneurial experience as the monetary profit. A major element in the non-monetary reward may consist of a long-term impact on the society. As a keen student of Japanese business history has pointed out, entrepreneurs 'not only innovate economically but reshape parts of the prevailing social orders'.[20] Even though social impact may be an unintended by-product of the forces that an enterprise may set in motion, its significance for analysing entrepreneurial behaviour is, nevertheless, great. Admittedly, social content cannot be easily measured, but then entrepreneurship itself is an immeasurable phenomenon. The best we can hope to do is to have an intellectual scale to help us arrive at a qualitative judgement.

With the conceptual issues out of our way, let us now turn to reviews of Japanese and Indian experiences in industrial entrepreneurship in the light of the *schema* outlined above. The first relevant question to be examined is: What were the respective constellations of forces in these two countries when they launched their first successful experiments in factory based, modern type industries? Let us take up the case of Japan first.

NOTES

1. Most works relating to comparative entrepreneurship fall in two broad categories: (i) those which have used comparative data for developing entrepreneurial theories—such as Hugh G.H. Aitkin (ed.), *Explorations in Enterprise*, based on the researches conducted by the Harvard Research Center in Entrepreneurial History during 1948-57 (Cambridge: Harvard University Press, 1965); David C. McClleland, *The Achieving Society* (Princeton: Princeton University Press. 1961); Everette E. Hagen, *On the Theory of Social Change* (Homewood Ill.: Dorsey Press, 1962) and (ii) those which are mainly concerned with comparative economic growth such as Simon Kuznets, *et al.* (eds.), *Economic Growth: Brazil, India, Japan* (Durham: Duke University Press, 1955); Cyril E. Black, *et al.*, *The Modernization of Japan and Russia: A Comparative Study* (New York: Free Press, 1975), Kazushi Okhawa and Gustav Ranis (eds.), *Japan and the Developing Countries: A Comparative Analysis* (New York: Basil Blackwell, 1985); Alexander Gerschenkron, *Economic Backwardness in Historical Perspective* (Cambridge: Mass., Belknop Press, 1962) and *Continuity in History and Other Essays* (Cambridge: Harvard University Press, 1968), S. Ishikawa, *Economic Development in Asian Perspective* (Tokyo: Kinokuniya, 1967); The multi-volume proceedings of the Fuji Conference in Business History published by the Tokyo University Pr. s, Tokyo, since 1976 are mainly concerned with Japan but contain some comparative insight. Of particular interest in this series is Keiichiro Nakagawa (ed.), *Social Order and Entrepreneurship* (Tokyo: Tokyo University Press, 1977). A few articles pertaining to comparative analysis of entrepreneurial behaviour in different countries are cited at appropriate places in this essay.
2. V.V. Bhatt, *Aspects of Economic Change and Policy in India, 1800-1960* (Bombay: Allied Publishers, 1963), p. 60. For the early progress of Indian cotton industry see S.D. Mehta, *Cotton Mills of India, 1854-1954* (Bombay: Textile Association, 1954), pp. 13-22. The beginning of cotton industry in Japan has been discussed in G.C. Allen, *A Short Economic History of Modern Japan* (London: George Allen and Unwin, 1968), pp. 71-2.
3. Bhatt, *Aspects of Economic Change . . .* , p. 70.

4. Discussing railway development in India, Daniel Thorner wrote: 'The foreign orientation of India's economic life and the wasteful use of her limited resources stand in sharp contrast to the domestic orientation of Japan's economy and the careful husbanding of the limited capital available to the Japanese. The difference in the pattern of evolution of the two countries is certainly not attributable to a single factor like railway policy. Rather the difference in railway policy illustrates the difference in the direction and emphasis between a country running its own affairs and a dependency whose affairs were being managed by an external power.' *The Shaping of Modern India* (New Delhi: Allied Publishers, 1980), p. 123. At another place he has referred to the lack of 'any major attempt to improve output [of agriculture] as for example was the case in Meiji Japan'. Danial and Alice Thorner, 'Long-term Trands in Output' in Dainel Thorner, *Land and Labour in India* (Bombay: Asia Publishing House, 1962), p. 111. Some other important works in this genere are: Bipan Chandra, *The Rise and Growth of Economic Nationalism in India* (New Delhi: People's Publishing House, 1979); Amiya K. Bagchi, *Private Investment in India, 1900-1939* (Cambridge: Cambridge University Press, 1972); Sumit Sarkar, *Modern India, 1885-1947* (New Delhi: Macmillan, 1985). Morris D. Morris, 'Towards Reinterpretation of the 19th Century Indian Economic History', *Journal of Economic History*, Vol. 23, No. 4 (Dec. 1963), was probably the most daring attempt to correct this widespread notion. For its critique see a series of articles in *Indian Economic and Social History Review*, Vol. 5, No. 4 (Dec. 1968).
5. The works attributing India's backwardness to its socio-cultural values are galore. Most prominent among these are Max Weber. *Religion of India: The Sociology of Hinduism and Buddhism*, trans. and ed. by H.H. Gerth and D. Martindale (Glenco, Ill.: Free Press, 1958); L.C.A. Knowles, *The Economic Development of British Overseas Empire* (London: George & Routledge, 1928), Vol. I, p. 2; K. William Kapp, *Hindu Culture, Economic Development and Economic Planning in India* (New York: Asia Publishing House, 1963). For critiques of this approach, Morris D. Morris, 'Values as an Obstacle to Economic Growth in South Asia: An Historical Survey', *Journal of Economic History*, Vol. 27, No. 4 (December 1967); Dwijendra Tripathi, 'Occupational Mobility and Industrial Entrepreneurship in India: A Historical Analysis', *Developing Economies*, Vol. 19, No. 1 (March 1981).
6. H.J. Habakkuk, 'The Historical, Experience on the Basic Conditions of Economic Progress' in *Economic Progress*, ed. by Leon H. Dupriez (Louvain: Institute de Recherches Ecojomiqueset Sociales, 1955), pp. 149-69.

7. For a flavour see a series of articles in *Entrepreneurship: The Japanese Experience* (a ten-volume journal published between March 1982 and June 1985 by the PHP Institute, Kyoto, specifically for the benefit of non-Japanese readers) which illustrate the popular view of Japanese culture being the engine of economic change. A scholarly representative of this school is S. Ishikawa, *Economic Development in Asian Perspective*; also M. Morishima, *The Economic Theory of Modern Society* (Cambridge: The University Press, 1976), pp. 299-304. At the prestigious Tokyo colloquium in 1985, *nihonjin-ron* was repeatedly referred to by several participants.
8. Morris D. Morris has hinted this in his 'South Asian Entrepreneurship and the Rashomon Effect', *Explorations in Economic History*, Vol. 16, No. 1 (July 1979), p. 346. He, however, does not develop his arguments.
9. For a fuller discussion see Simon Kuznets, 'Problems in Comparisons of Economic Trends' in *Economic Growth: Brazil. India, Japan*, ed. by Simon Kuznets, *et al.*, pp. 3-28.
10. For a brilliant argument on this see Richard G. Fox, *Lions of the Punjab: Culture in the Making* (Berkeley: University of California Press, 1985); the quote is from p. 197.
11. For the all-pervasive influence of Hinduism see Max Weber, *Religion of India*, pp. 18-20.
12. Perhaps the most telling example of this is a book written by a Japanese and published a few years before the beginning of recent resurgence of the Japanese economy. The writer was a highly placed official in the Japanese government and was a member of a study team which had gone to the United State around 1950. He wrote the book after his return, condemning almost every aspect of Japanese life in relation to economic activities. See Ichiro Kawasaki, *Japanese are Like That* (Rutland Vt.: C.E. Tuttle, 1955).
13. For a more detailed discussion see Dwijendra Tripathi, 'An Integrated View of Entrepreneurship', *Economic and Political Weekly*, Review of Management, Vol. 20, No. 48 (30 Nov. 1985).
14. Arthur H. Cole, *Business Enterprise in Its Social Setting* (Cambridge: Harvard University Press, 1959), p. 7.
15. Jean B. Say, *A Treatise on Political Economy* (New York: A.M. Kelley, 1964, first published in French in 1803), p. 295; also his *Catechism of Political Economy* (London: Sherwood, 1816), pp. 28-9.
16. Joseph A. Schumpeter, *Theory of Economic Development* (Cambridge: Harvard University Press, 1934), p. 55; also see his 'Creative Response in Economic History, *Journal of Economic History*, Vol. 7, No. 2 (Nov. 1947).
17. David C. McClleland, *The Achieving Society* (Princeton: Van Nostrand 1961), Chap. 3.

18. Gustav Schmoller, 'The Historical Development of the Enterprise' in *Enterprise and Secular Change*, a collection of articles written during 1890-3 and edited by Frederick C. Lane (Homewood, Ill.: Irwin, 1953), p. 6; Arthur H. Cole, 'An Approach to the Study of Entrepreneurship', *Journal of Economic History*, Vol. 6, Supplement (1946), p. 7.
19. Schumpeter seems to have inspired this dichotomy, albeit unwittingly. But while he used the terms 'creative response' and 'adaptive response' to distinguish between decisions taken within existing range of options available in *an* economy and those falling outside this range (see his essay 'Creative Response . . .', p. 150, some later writers have applied these terms to differentiate the experience of early industrialisers from that of the latecomers. See for instance, Yusif A. Sayigh, *Entrepreneurs of Lebanon* (Cambridge: Harvard University Press, 1962), pp. 19-20; James H. Berna, *Industrial Entrepreneurship in Madras State* (Bombay: Asia Publishing House, 1960), p. 6, P.B. Medhora, 'Entrepreneurship in India', *Political Science Quarterly*, Vol. 30, No. 4 (Dec. 1965), pp. 558-80; D.P. Pandit, 'Creative Response in Indian Economy: A Regional Analysis', *Economic Weekly*, Vol. 9, No. 9 (2 March 1957), p. 317.
20. J. Hirschmeier, 'Entrepreneurs and the Social Order: America, Germany, and Japan', in *Social Order and Entrepreneurship*, ed. by K. Nakagawa (Tokyo: University of Tokyo Press, 1977), p. 3.

CHAPTER II

Japan: The Seed Time

COTTON TEXTILE has marked the beginning of industrial transformation almost in every country in the world. It may be due to the fact that this industry, depending on agriculture for its basic raw material, did not represent a sharp break from manufacturing processes prevailing previously. In Japan, too, it was the cotton textile that heralded the modern method of industrial production. The credit for establishing the first mill, using modern machinery, in this island country goes to the lord of Satsuma. He set up his first factory in 1867, followed by a second mill three years later. Japan's third cotton mill was born in 1872 when a merchant, named Kashima Mampei, emulated the feudal chief's example.[1] Thus the first venture that marked the beginning of a new age in the industrial history of Japan preceded the Meiji Restoration (1868), commonly regarded as the major catalyst of socio-economic revolution in the land of the rising sun. This means that the Restoration did not initiate, though it unquestionably reinforced, as we shall see later, the process of creating the pre-conditions conducive to the emergence of industrial entrepreneurship.

What were those pre-conditions and how did they develop?

I

The most conspicuous feature of Japan in 1868 was a remarkable degree of political unity. The process of unification had started as early as in the middle of the sixteenth century under Oda Nobunaga (1534-82) and was carried forward by Toyotomi Hideyoshi (1536-98). But it was the Tokugawa dynasty founded by Iyeyasu (1598-1616) which completed the task. Whatever its other faults, the Tokugawa Shogunate, acting in the name of the emperor but in reality exercising despotic authority over the country, succeeded in subjugating a large number of local feudal lords (*daimyo*) to create a nation out of what before 1603 was nothing but a group of desparate and scattered territories, entirely independent of one another and owing only theoretical allegiance to the distant and invisible emperor.

Even though the Tokugawas' direct management was limited to the Shogunal domains (*tenryo*) and some of the principal commercial cities, the managerial and administrative practices followed by them provided the model for the local *daimyos* to govern their own territories (*hans*). Admittedly, the common man had little to do with the central government (*Bakufu*), but the supreme power that the Shogunate exercised in the entire length and breadth of the land for more than 250 years served to cement the national unity the like of which the country had never experienced before.

The task of political integration was rendered still easier because the land was inhabited, by and large, by people of a common racial stock who spoke a common language. There of course, were groups like *Ainus* and *Eta* who remained outside the mainstream. The former were a people of mysterious origin who had been living in the northern islands of Honshu and Hokaido since much before the ancestors of the Japanese set foot on the soil. With their distinctive physical features they were easily recognizable, they spoke a different language, and their socio-cultural norms too were different. The Eta (literally meaning 'people of filth') were ethnically Japanese but were looked down upon because they ate meat and worked as butchers, gravediggers and leatherworkers. The number of both these groups, however, was too small to hinder the process of the national integration.

Political unification of the country was not the only achievement of the Tokugawas. They also established unprecedented internal peace which the nation continued to enjoy throughout the period of their hegemony. True, there were several peasant uprisings between 1600 and 1868—about 1000 according to a rough reckoning—but these were nothing in comparison with the continual strifes which had ravaged the land throughout its previous history. Moreover, all these revolts were local in character. Some were directed either against the maladministration of local officials or reflected the scornful attitude of the townsman towards the rural farmer; a few originated in religious frictions: but a majority of them were caused by discontent engendered by the policies of the landowners.

These sporadic incidents might have supplemented, in final analysis, the causes of the eventual downfall of the *Bakufu*, but in themselves they created only minor ripples in the general air of national tranquillity, and generated little disaffection against the central authority. And as the Shogunate was believed to be speaking for and acting in the name of the God-incarnate emperor, regarded universally as the fountainhead of all powers—temporal as well as ecclesiastical—political integration and internal peace had a great deal of significance for national goal-setting, particularly if the general populace claimed a common racial origin and spoke a common language. In short, the Tokugawas succeeded in creating not only a unified nation but also a cohesive society.[2]

The Tokugawa regime had taken several steps to buttress its undisputed sway over the nation. One of these was the system of *sankin-kotai* which can roughly be translated as 'alternate reporting for audience'. Under this system, every *daimyo* was required to spend some time, normally one out of every two years, in personal attendance at the Shogunal court in Edo (the pre-Restoration name of Tokyo), the headquarter of the central government. The purpose was to make sure that the *daimyos* did not become unduly strong, politically and economically. The system led to the development of a fairly extensive transportation network in the country as every *han* had to be linked with the capital city. True, the roads were narrow and unpaved, and the Tokugawa authorities discouraged construction of bridges, but there is no doubt that during their rule, there was a vast improvement in the facilities for internal movement. At the same time coastal shipping routes were established and extended from the inland sea to Edo and from Hokaido to the inland sea. Nearly 75 per cent of Japan's surface is covered by hills and mountains, where road construction would not have been easy. But few countries in Asia could then boast of better means of internal transport, or even close to what Japan developed during this period. Such was the importance the Tokugawa authorities attached to facilitating movement in their dominion—or such were the political compulsions on them—to link various parts of the country with one another.[3]

Among other measures taken by the Tokugawas to consolidate their hegemony was the abolition of the custom barriers (*sekisho*) which had continued to multiply, reflecting the political dismemberment of the country, throughout the long span of

Japanese history up to the middle of the sixteenth century. Then Nobunaga initiated a policy of destroying them relentlessly which his successor pursued with still greater vigour. Under the Tokugawas, private construction of *sekisho* was prohibited and those which existed functioned purely as police outposts, instead of commercial checkposts, to keep an eye on possible rebels. The period also witnessed the standardization of weights and measures and stabilizing of the currency system. Reform in both these spheres had been initiated in the latter half of the sixteenth century before the emergence of the Tokugawas on the political scene. Nobunaga is credited to have issued the first legal tender in gold, and Hideyoshi took the first steps towards eliminating variations in the methods of weighing and measuring things. It was, however, left to Iyeyasu to complete the process begun by his predecessors.

Particularly impressive was his achievement in unifying and stablilizing the currency system. When Iyeyasu came to power, a host of currencies were circulating in the country along with the Tonsho Oban—the gold coin which Nobunaga had declared to be the legal tender. There were gold, silver and copper coins of varying denominations issued by a multitude of local lords. Some reputable merchant houses also minted coins as there was no central control over the mints. Merchant houses issued lumps of gold dust with their values marked on the paper packages. These, too, were freely used in transaction. The absence of a uniform exchange rate between one kind of currency and the other made the confusion worse confounded.

Iyeyasu not only declared the Oban as the legal tender throughout the land but also divided it into ten fractions, called *ryos*, which became the basic unit of value. He effected similar reforms in silver and copper based currencies and introduced fixed exchange rates. His greatest achievement, however, was to establish central monopoly on mints and abolish private coinage altogether. His successors continued and consolidated his currency policy, with the result that by the end of the seventeenth century the currency system of the land was reasonably well unified.[4]

All this served to expand the size of the market. As the country was politically integrated and various restraints on trade—such as custom barriers, multiplicity of weights and measure and currency confusion—were either eliminated or considerably weakened, it was now possible for a merchant to conduct business over a much larger area. Likewise, the expansion of transportation network coupled with the security of movement, that a strong government and internal peace provided, opened up new vistas for business. It is no surprise, therefore, that the merchant class, though placed at the bottom of the social hierarchy as we shall see later, thrived and prospered even though it was not trade but agriculture that was officially patronized. the Tokugawas dictum *kikoku-senkin* ('revere grain, despise money') could not stop the economic laws from operating.

Apart from the physical changes outlined above, there were other factors which aided this development. One was the revenue system of the Tokugawa era. Consistent with the feudal character of the regime, land tax formed the most important source of its revenue. With only minor variations, the state—*Bakufu* and the *daimyos* together—claimed about 40 to 50 per cent of the produce in taxes which the central government and local chiefs shared in certain proportions. This was to be paid to the *daimyo*, in whose *han* the territory fell. In theory, the tax could be paid in cash or kind, but in actual practice a large part was paid in kind—largely rice which was the staple crop.[5] As the feudal lord needed a less cumbersome medium of exchange than rice to run the administration of his fief and to finance his biennial attendance at the Shogunal court, he had to depend on the services of the merchants to convert his grain wealth into cash. This provided a new function and a new source of profit to the merchant class.

This, however, was not the only link between the financial and the ruling elite and those who controlled the money power. Very often, the *daimyo* found it difficult to make both ends meet out of his tax revenue. In such cases, he had to turn to the merchant who offered financial accommodation against future deliveries of grain at 15 to 20 per cent annual rate of interest. Significantly enough, not only the *han* leaders but the *Bakufu* as well depended on the services the merchants offered. It is not surprising, therefore, that they were granted various kinds of privileges by the *daimyos* and the *Shogunate* alike. It is one of the ironies of history that the merchant class emerged in gradual stages as the lynchpin in the financial wheel of a political system which was explicitly committed to the physiocratic conception of the economy.

The merchant's involvement in rendering the *daimyo's* collection into something amenable to easier exchange or advancing him funds in hours of need had significant consequences for the character and organization of internal commerce. As the grain could not be allowed to rot in warehouses, inter-regional trade developed, opportunities for foreign commerce being restricted thanks to *Bakufu's* policy of *sakoku* (closing of the country against contact with other lands) which was rigidly enforced after 1639. This brought to the fore a new class of trader—known as *tonya*—who specialized in wholesale business not only in grain but also other commodities. To facilitate transmission of funds over long distances, the use of various types of credit instruments such as bills of exchange and promissory notes became much more common than before and the more prominent dealers in money opened their branches in different parts of the country. Specialization developed and guild-type organizations—*kabu nakama*—to regulate trade in various lines emerged on the commercial landscape.[6] As a cumulative consequence of all this, the economy of the land was almost completely monetized.[7]

Growth in commerce coupled with an ever-rising population led to the growth of urban centres both in size and number. Some of the older cities such as Edo, Osaka, and Kyoto developed into large metropolis. At the same time new cities emerged where formerly nothing but small farming or fishing hamlets existed. The growth of urban centres was partly a result of unprecedented attention given to building castle towns (*jokamachi*) by the *shogun* and the *daimyos*. So fast was this development that the period between 1550 and 1610 may be regarded as that of a veritable urban revolution in Japan without a parallel in world history. Even though their erection was necessitated by military and administrative needs of a feudal order, the *jokamachis* soon became busy centres of economic activity with all the hustle and bustle that characterized the purely commercial cities. The *daimyos* reinforced the process by offering patronage and protection to the merchants in order to attract them to their headquarters. The implication of this development for business and capital accumulation can be easily understood.[8]

The cause of capital accumulation was also aided by developments on the agricultural front. There is a general con-sensus that the productivity of land increased considerably during the Tokugawa period, partly because of the reclamation of vast tracts of land which resulted in substantial expansion of the area under cultivation. According to a rough estimate, the area of cultivable land almost doubled between 1600 and 1720. The peasant economy, however, escaped the possible disastrous effect of over-production because there was simultaneously a welcome increase in the range of crops produced. Instead of concentrating on producing foodgrains alone, as was the case before, the peasant began to pay increasingly greater attention to growing cash crops such as cotton, oil-seeds, tea, indigo, sugar, silkworms, etc. Beginning with the early eighteenth century, there was a definite trend toward diversification and commercialization of agriculture. The result was that market demand rather than the limited need to feed the local population began to influence the choice of crops the peasant sowed. In other words, market economy replaced purely subsistence agriculture to a certain extent.

Rising productivity and growing commercialization of agriculture produced two significant results for the rural economy of the country. One, the peasant was left with an increasingly larger surplus. For, the quantum of land tax, fixed at the end of the sixteenth century following the survey of land conducted during the reign of Hideyoshi, changed only marginally and that too perhaps downward, while other taxes, collectively known as *komononari*, were too insignificant to make material difference. And secondly, this surplus was available to the cultivator in cash rather than in kind. A part of this surplus was invested in trading and moneylending and for setting up manufacturing enterprises based on agricultural commodities—cotton and silks-spinning, sake-brewing, miso- and soy-sauce making, paper and *tatami* production, etc. Growing prosperity of the peasants and the development of rural trade and industry attracted the attention of city merchants and traditional peddlers, such as those belonging to Omi and Ise regions, who began to partake of the new, emerging opportunities for profit in the countryside. This resulted in the linking of rural and urban commerce and the rise of a new class of rural bourgeoisie. There is no doubt that the Japansese agriculture by the end of the Tokugawa era had developed many essential features of primitive capitalism.[9]

Capitalistic development of agriculture, of course, did not benefit all peasants equally. The less enterprising among them were left behind in the race. Many incurred heavy debts, offering their lands as collateral and eventually losing effective control over them to their creditors—usually rich peasants or merchants. Also those parts of the country where climate and soil were more favourable and which were closer to major commercial or consumption centres, such as Osaka, Edo, and Kyoto, felt a greater impact of capitalistic formation than the areas which were poorly endowed in these respects. This explains the differential development of the Kansai region in the south-west of Japan, which became a thriving centre of the rural and urban bourgeoisies, and the less fortunate north-east.

II

The upshot of the above discussion is that the changes in the physical environment wrought during the Tokugawa regime expanded the horizon of business and created new opportunities for profit. This period in Japanese history also witnessed significant new developments on the ideational side of the constellation of forces. The most conspicuous shift was from the Buddhist emphasis on otherworldliness to a more secular ideology embodied in Neo-Confucian doctrines.[11] True, Buddhism did not disappear from Japanese life, and most Tokugawa rulers ostensibly remained ardent patrons of this faith. None, at any rate, emulated Nobunaga in persecuting the Buddhist clergy and destroying monasteries. But the Buddhist theology—any theology for that matter—never took deep roots in the country, and Japanese polity resembled, in the words of Jean-Pierre Lehman, a 'secular theocracy'[12] in which 'national sovereignty involves both spiritual and political powers'.[13] Under these situations, official espousal of Neo-Confucianism was bound to have profound impact on the social norm and behaviour.

The process was further accelerated by the way the Japanese philosophers interpreted the principles of the Chinese masters. They saw no contradiction between Neo-Confucianism and the Buddhist and Shinto doctrines. They emphasized commonalities and underplayed differences. Their synthesizing can perhaps best be summarized in the words of a late Tokugawa philosopher:

> Shinto is the Way which provides for the foundation of the country; Confucianism is the Way which provides for governing the country: Buddhism is the Way which provides for governing one's mind. Caring no more for lofty speculation than the humble truth, I have tried simply to

extract the essence of each of these teachings. By essence I mean their importance to mankind. Selecting what is important and discarding what is unimportant. I have arrived at the best teaching for mankind, which I call the teaching of Repaying Virtue. I also call it the 'pill containing the essence of Shintoism, Confucianism and Buddhism'.[14]

Admittedly, there was much in the Neo-Confucian doctrines which seemed to run counter to the spirit of commerce. A hierarchical basis of the society, stress on strict obedience of the higher order by the lower, a sort of all-pervasive paternalism embracing the nation at every level, and a powerful accent on a neat, dull orderliness of the world—these were unlikely to disturb the social and economic equilibrium or create an aggressive, independent personality capable of branching out into new and untried directions. The Neo-Confucianism, however, was primarily and essentially concerned with the material or physical world—its substantiality and intelligibility in contrast to the Buddhist emphasis on its evanescence or release from its bonds. Pointing to reason and human experience as the basic sources of laws governing man's behaviour, the Neo-Confucianism had a sort of liberating influence on the Japanese mind, somewhat similar to the impact of the Renaissance on European social ethos. Pursuit of material happiness as a consequence attained a much greater respectability than had been the case before.

The Tokugawa espousal of the Neo-Confucian doctrine was not due to its material content but because of its stress on social harmony and order which they needed more than anything else to nourish the legitimacy to their authority. The organization of the society based on four estates—*shi no ko sho* or samurai, peasants, artisans and merchants—had the same purpose behind it. The samurai or the warrior estate, indispensable for the protection of the *bakuhan* system of government, was at the apex of the social order and enjoyed a number of privileges which were denied to the members of the other three estates. The samurai, at the same time, was to be the standard bearer of social morality. He was, therefore, subject to a series of moral injunctions, contained in an elaborate code of conduct known as the *bushido* (the way of the *bushi*, an equivalent term for samurai). The code enjoined upon him to lead a life of frugality and austerity and shun any kind of mercantile or other economic pursuits including agriculture. His sole source of subsistence was the stipends of rice he received from his lord in lieu of the services rendered. Any deviation from the prescribed norm invited severe punishment.[15]

Although the *bushido* was meant expressly for the samurai class, it had a profound influence on the behaviour pattern of the members of the other three estates. In a basically feudal order, it is the ruling elite that normally sets the tone of social norms. This phenomenon can be observed in the history of other countries as well. But in Tokugawa Japan where the distinction between the sources of moral and political powers was extremely blurred if not entirely non-existent, and where looking up to the superior order was considered to be a virtue thanks to the impact of Neo-Confucian doctrines, it was natural for the people at the lower rungs to try to emulate those at the top in the day-to-day conduct. Perhaps, this trend was further reinforced by the Tokugawa policy of *sakoku* which precluded the possibility, for more than two handred years, of external influences disturbing the lower orders' emulation of the social and moral ideals of their superiors.

Moreover, the adherence to the *bushido* norms by the non-*bushi* strata was not entirely left to the natural process of diffusion. A number of official injunctions applicable to the members of other estates served as formidable barriers against the temptation on their part to transgress the code. The *chonin* or the city dwellers, for instance, could indulge in profligacy, luxury and conspicuous consumption only at the cost of official patronage—a cost that a generally despised group, particularly under an essentially totalitarian regime, could not easily afford. The result was that the *bushido* came to be regarded as the embodiment of social norms and ideals cherished by all and sundry in the nation and not only by its primary target group.

This is not to suggest that the values sanctified in the *bushido* were fully internalized by the Tokugawa society and the gap between the actual social conduct and the desirable social values was entirely eliminated. No society in history has ever been able to do so and Japan, despite the oft-repeated claim to uniqueness, was no exception. Instances of deviation from *bushido* values not only by the ordinary folks but also by the exalted samurai, who was to be a role model for others, can be multiplied to illustrate the gulf that existed between the prescribed and actual social behaviour. It must be remembered, however, that unlike many other societies social sanction was not the only force behind the *bushido* values;

the weight of official machinery to enforce these values made deviations much more difficult, much more hazardous.

While the violations of certain norms, such as those regarding sexual morality, could go undetected and therefore unpunished, transgression of prescriptions regarding frugality and austerity would have been easily noticed, inviting official wrath. The result was that austere living, saving habit, and avoidance of conspicuous consumption, forced by governmental fiat to begin with, became a part of the Japanese social ethos with the passage of time. Not that these norms were always scrupulously adhered to, but the exceptions seem to point to what must be considered a general behaviour pattern. Providing additional enforcement to these virtues were the economic and geographical forces. The state of the Japanese economy during the Tokugawa period did not permit much luxuries for the general populace and, in a country given to frequent natural disasters like earthquakes and typhoons, it was quite human for people to think of possible rainy days while husbanding their resources even in sunny weather.

The impact of the *bushido* on Japanese life was not confined to inculcating these economic virtues alone: it also influenced the managerial structure of business firms. As the law of the samurai came to be regarded as a model for all relationships in Japan, the business structure gradually became a sort of microcosm of the ideal of the *han*. A typical business establishment was organized around the concept of *ie,* certain essential features of which are reflected in Japanese management even today. The closest English equivalent of this Japanese term is 'family', but *ie* encompasses much more, and consanguinity was not its most important characteristic. A commercial *ie* consisted of a head and a group of employees or dependents who, though not related by blood, were bound to one another by a sense of belonging in roughly the same manner as the members of an extended family. Their conduct and behaviour were informed by a set of unspecified moral obligations as in the case of samurai and *daimyo* in a typical *han* organization. And like a family or *han* structure, the *ie* was rigidly hierarchical in character.

Apprenticeship was the most common door for entry into an *ie*. The apprentice (*deshi*), usually entered the organization at a young age, was bound by complete loyalty to the head of the firm, received no wages except free boarding and lodging, and had very little freedom to do anything but serve the firm. His only gain was that he learnt a craft, skill, or trade which he could not have done otherwise, and his hope was that, if his mentor was pleased with his performance after a long period of probation, he would be admitted as a full-fledged member of the *ie*, guaranteeing life-long employment.

A successful apprenticeship usually led to the position of journeyman (*tedai*) and then to that of a manager (*banto*). An exceptionally competent *banto* could even hope to become the head of the *ie*. In that case he would probably be adopted as an heir and marry a daughter of the head of the *ie*. In many cases the competence and performance of a successful *banto* was rewarded by permitting him to establish a branch (*bekke*) of the firm with the start-up capital provided by the head office (*honke*). His loyalty to the main branch, however, must remain unimpaired or else he would not only forfeit the right to *bekke*, but also expose himself to eternal shame and social disgrace.

The *ie*, thus, was neither just a family nor a mere business enterprise. It was both merged into one and its continued prosperity and growth was the concern of everyone in the organization, no matter what his position was or whether he was related to the head by blood or otherwise. Ensuring the continuity of the *ie*, like the continuity of an ordinary family line, was of paramount importance. Should this objective so demand, considerations of blood could be disregarded while deciding the succession and a capable *banto* unrelated to the head could be chosen to follow him in the leadership role. In that case he would adopt the family name by which the *ie*, was known and assume the responsibility of protecting not only the business interest of the firm but also the fair name of the progenitors of his adopted family exactly as a natural heir would have done. The example of this kind of management system based on total paternalism would be hard to find anywhere else in the world. It flourished in Japan, because it conformed to the prevailing feudal structure of the society on one hand and the basic familial values on the other.[16] Nothing perhaps was considered a greater virtue than maintaining the family line and furthering the legacy of the ancestors.[17]

If the policy of *sakoku*, as has been pointed out earlier, had much to do with the consolidation of some of the distinctive features of the social and economic life of Japan, the seclusion of the country for more than two hundred years also seems to have encouraged experimentation in broadening the technological base. At a time when opportunities for agricultural pursuits were expanding and contact with external technology was not easily possible, the only way to facilitated the exploitation of new opportunities was to improve the indigenous know-how. It is no surprise, therefore, that the Tokugawa Japan gave rise to a numerous class of publicists for whom this became the primary concern. Unlike the Neo-Confucian philosophers, who were more interested in theoretical discussion on social and political issues, these writers—Thomas C. Smith calls them 'technologists'—were primarily concerned with mundane, practical problems. For them economic progress was more important, and economic progress was possible only through the application of better methods in forestry, sericulture, mining, sugar manufacturing and the use of improved seeds, fertilizers, and agricultural implements.

The technologists took upon themselves the task of discovering these methods and equipments and disseminating their discoveries through their writings. Whether and to what extent their precepts were acted upon is difficult to determine, but this is beside the point. The existence of a large body of applied literature concerned with the practical problems of agriculture and industry suggests that there was a fairly widespred interest in such matters among the Japanese masses.[18] It also suggests that the Japanese society had developed a certain degree of confidence in its ability to grapple with and improve the available technology.

The development and diffusion of new processes and methods through the works of the technologists was due, among other things, to a fairly high level of literacy in the Tokugawa Japan. For several reasons, the *bakuhan* authorities considered it expedient to encourage education. It provided a useful outlet for the energies of the samurai, who had very little work to do during the long period of peace. Education was also considered necessary to inculcate among the commoners the virtue of social harmony. Above all, the Neo-Confucian principles laid a great deal of stress on the value of formal learning. Formal education, therefore, received a great deal of fillip under the Tokugawas and a number of institutions were established for this purpose. According to a competent estimate, about half the Japanese population had received some form of formal education or at least could read and write.

This means that pursuit of learning was not confined to the elite; it percolated down to every strata of the society. Significantly enough, practically all technologists were educated in more or less degree and none belonged to the ruling class. All of them were 'mostly obscure men—farmers, merchants and small manufacturers—who never held high office and generally lived out their lives in villages and small towns'. Even more important than the high rate of literacy was the fact that education during the Edo era became completely secular, inculcating rational, even critical, faculties consistent with the emphasis in the Confucian doctrines. Even though the schools for the commoners (*heimin*) continued to be called *terakoya* (temple schools), as they had been called previously, the accent in their curriculum was on three Rs rather than religious instruction.[19]

The expansion and secularization of education coupled with the Confucian emphasis on 'thisworldliness' was bound to create a more questioning spirit in a society where the impact of religious theology was never too pronounced. The process was further aided by the infiltration of Western learning from the small port of Dejima in the Nagasaki Bay where the Dutch had been allowed to maintain a modest establishment. Although the Dutch Studies (*Rangaku*) made little headway for almost a century after the rise of the Tokugawa hegemony, the *bakufu* developed a more tolerant attitude towards Western learning after 1716 when the ban on foreign books was partially lifted. The study of Western arts and sciences consequently evoked much greater interest during the remaining century and a half of the Tokugawa hegemony.

Admittedly, only a small circle of academic elite could afford the time and resources to study Western subjects, but the Japanese experts in Europology must have served as an effective vehicle to spread their knowledge and understanding to the general populace. Also, even though most of the works which attracted the attention of Japanese scholars pertained to applied fields rather than the realm of ideas and thoughts, they were sufficient to provide at least a limited understanding of some facets of European life and society. The liberalizing influence of Western learning, thus, on the Japanese mind should not be underestimated.[20]

It would have been a miracle indeed if the social division in Japan, as represented by *shi-no-ko-sho*, had remained intact in the face of all these developments. The Tokugawas had virtually 'frozen' the society as they found it at the beginning of their power and intended to keep it that way. This means that even a slight deviation from the *shi-no-ko-sho* scheme was strictly forbidden. For a samurai, particularly, embracing any remunerative occupation or marrying a girl from other estates was tantamount to commit-ting an unpardonable crime. And yet as the infrastructural changes wrought during the Tokugawa regime consolidated themselves, the horizon of business opportunities expanded. At the same time, the new cultural and educational influences loosened to some extent the hold of tradition and dogma on the Japanese mind. As a result of these twin factors the urge for social and occupational mobility began to erode the social regimentation imposed by the political fiat. In other words, the neat equilibrium between the social division and occupational choices sanctified by the tradition and enforced by the government of the day began to experience severe strain. While some signs of this were visible even earlier, the process of change became much more pronounced during the closing decades of the *bakuhan* system.

Ironically, it was the samurai class, supposedly the protectors of the *status quo,* which seems to have been most seduced by the forces of change. Most samurai were beneficiaries of superior education, and their economic position, particularly of those belonging to the lower ranks, was constantly deteriorating since the middle of the eighteenth century, even as the solvency of their mentor *daimyos* was fast declining. It is not at all surprising, therefore, that some of these samurai were the first to grasp the significance of the emerging economic opportunities for their own material salvation, and take advantage of them even if it meant the loss of their exalted social status. The result was a spiralling increase in the number of *ronin* (masterless samurai) who chose to sever their traditional connection with their *daimyos* to set off on a new course. Some of these moved into business, defying the official injunctions. Fearing the consequences, some of these traitors to the cause of samurai purity kept the downward shift in their occupation a closely guarded secret.

Significantly enough, at least two prominent mercantile firms in the Tokugawa Japan developed out of samurai initiative. Shinemon Shinroku, the founder of the House of Konoike, and his successors who consolidated the fortunes of this premier sake brewing firm, kept their samurai background concealed and identified themselves with the merchant class. Likewise, Hachirobe Takatoshi laid the foundation of the Mitsui dynasty in the seventeenth century despite being the son of a samurai.[21] If the samurai, who were supposed to hold aloft the torch of *shi-no-ko-sho*, were lured by the corrupting temptation of economic gain, the impact of the forces of change on others can be easily surmised.

Official injunctions against social and occupational mobility, however, remained. Agriculture continued to be praised and business despised. Various kind of disabilities imposed on the merchant class were never formally withdrawn. Though there were some reformers who seemed to appreciate the emerging trends, business as a profession continued to be held in low public esteem, the profit motive despised, and profit-makers frequently ridiculed. These factors in Japanese society must have held back to some extent the resurgent spirit of enterprise.

The forces of *status quo*, nevertheless, were fighting a losing battle against the forces of change. The combined impact of the positive developments of the Tokugawa period—emergence of a cohesive nation and a national market, improvement in transportation system, a long unbroken period of national unity and internal peace, elimination of threats and hurdles in the movement of goods and people, acceptance of frugality and thrift as general social virtues facilitating accumulation of capital, evolution of a management system conforming to the basic social values and structure, widespread expansion of secular education and a value system emphasizing reason rather than dogma, and the development of skill to grapple with technology—created a new climate for enterprise, causing disequilibrium between perceivable economic opportunities and their actual exploitation.

This, of course, was not something that the Tokugawa authorities wanted to happen. Far from it. Expansion of business horizon was only an unintended by-product of a set of policies and programmes directed essentially to the preservation of an autocratic feudal order. Without question there was much in the Tokugawa totalitarianism which was vulgar, odious, and repulsive. This, however, does not detract from the fact that the *bakuhan* system, viewed comprehensively, laid down, though unwittingly, the foundation of industrial change in Japan. In fact so firm had this foundation become by the time the Tokugawa period came to an end that easy accessibility to the technology necessary for setting up modern industrial ventures was perhaps the only element that was missing in an otherwise favourable constellation of forces.

It is not without significance that the first cotton mill was set up in a region where it was possible to surmount the hurdles in importing machinery from abroad and that it was set up before the Meiji Restoration. Situated close to Nagasaki through which a limited commercial intercourse with other countries was permitted, Satsuma *han* became the first to have modern spinning mill, established under the patronage of the *daimyo* himself. The Meiji authorities, thus, inherited a society which was fully ripe for industrial transformation. In other words, the ground for sowing the seeds of industrial-economic 'take off' had already developed when the Tokugawas and their system of government were consigned to history.

NOTES

1. Keizo Seki, *The Cotton Industry of Japan* (Tokyo: Japan Society for the Promotion of Science, 1956), pp. 14-22.
2. For Tokugawa role in creating a unified and cohesive nation, see J.W. Hall, *Government and Local Power in Japan, 500 to 1700* (Princeton: Princeton University Press, 1966); H. Webb, *Japanese Imperial Institution in the Tokugawa Period* (New York: Columbia University Press, 1968); David N. Earl, *Emperor and Nation in Japan* (Seattle: University of Washington Press, 1964) and Arthur L. Sadler, *The Maker of Modern Japan: The Life of Tokugawa Iyeyasu, 1542-1616* (London: George Allen and Unwin, 1937); Hugh Borton, *Peasant Uprisings in Japan of the Tokugawa Period* (New York: Paragon Book Reprint Corp., 1968) is an excellent work on this aspect of Japanese history. E. Kaempfer, a German physician who visited Japan in the 1690s, was very impressed by the condition of roads and other communication facilities. See his *History of Japan* (New York: A.M.S. Press, 1978, rpt.).
3. For a detailed discussion, see T.G. Tsukahira, *Feudal Control in Tokugawa Japan: The Sankin-Kotai System* (Cambridge: Harvard University Press, 1970); also Peter Duus, *Feudalism in Japan* (New York: Alfred A. Knopf, 1969); and Jean-Pierre Lehmann, *The Roots of Modern Japan* (London: Macmillan, 1982), particularly Chap. 2
4. Yosoburo Takekoshi, *The Economic Aspects of the History of the Civilization of Japan* (London: Dawson of Pall Mall, 1967), Vol. I, pp. 381-414.

5. Ibid., pp. 415-40: Thomas C. Smith, 'The Land Tax in the Tokugawa Period', *Journal of Asian Studies*, Vol. 18, No. 1 (Nov. 1958).
6. Guilds or *za* which had existed in Japan since ancient times were abolished by Nobunaga but continued to function unofficially and were later granted official sanction in the last quarter of the seventeenth century. J. Hirschmeier and T. Yui, *Development of Japanese Business, 1600-1983* (London: George Allen and Unwin, 1985), pp. 36-8.
7. Letmann, *The Roots of Modern Japan*, pp. 64-79; Hirschmeier and Yui, *The Development of Japanese·Business. . .* , pp. 11-66; C.P. Sheldon, *The Rise of Merchant Class in Tokugawa Japan, 1600-1866* (New York: Russell & Russell, 1958). Captain Vasilii Galownin, a Russian captive in Japan in 1811-13, has testified to the evidence of 'the commercial spirit of the Japanese . . . in all the towns and villages'. See his *Memoirs of a Captivity in Japan* (London: Henry C. Colburn Co., 1824). pp. 82-94, 202-3.
8. J.W. Hall, 'The Castle Town and Japan's Modern Urbanization', *Far Eastern Quarterly*, Vol. 15, No. 1 (Nov. 1955).
9. Smith, 'Land Tax . . .'; see also his *The Agrarian Origins of Modern Japan* (Stanford: Stanford University Press, 1959); J. Hirschmeier, *The Origins of Entrepreneurship in Meiji Japan* (Cambridge: Harvard University Press, 1964), pp. 69-90.
10. William B. Hauser, *Economic Institutional Change in Tokugawa Japan* (Cambridge: Cambridge University Press, 1974), pp. 7-58.
11. R. Bellah, *Tokugawa Religion: The Values of Industrial Japan* (New York: Free Press, 1957); Ryusaku Tsunoda *et al.* (eds.), *Sources of Japanese Tradition* (New York: Columbia University Press, 1965), pp. 308-77.
12. Lehmann, *Roots of Modern Japan*, p. 114.
13. Maruyama Masao, *Thought and Behaviour in Modern Japanese Politics* (Oxford: Oxford University Press, 1963) quoted in Lehman, *Roots of Modern Japan*, p. 114.
14. Tsunoda *et al., Sources. . . .* , p. 585.
15. G.R. Storry, *The Way of the Samurai* (London: Orbis, 1978); Lehmann, *Roots of Modern Japan*, pp. 79-89; Hirschmeier, *The Origins of Entrepreneurship*, pp. 47-51.
16. J. Hirschmeier and Yui, *Development of Japanese Business . . . .* , pp. 38-43; also Lehmann, *Roots of Modern Japan*, pp. 76-8. Iwata in a widely read book written in the Japanese language has countered the popular view of the origin of Japanese style management and has argued that its roots lay in the Japanese village or local community. Shinichi Yonekawa, 'Recent Writing on Japanese Economic and Social History', *Economic History Review*, Second

Series, Vol. 38, No. 1 (February 1985), p. 116.

17. We may recall here that Emperor Hirohito while justifying surrender to the Allied forces during the Second World War referred to his obligation to his 'ancestors' to avoid the inevitable death of a large number of his subjects as a compelling factor for his decision.
18. Thomas C. Smith, 'Okura Nagatsune and the Technologists' in *Personality in Japanese History*, ed. by Albert M. Craig and D.H. Shively (Berkeley: University of California Press, 1970), pp. 127-54.
19. Ibid., p. 127, for quotation about technologists: Maries B. Jansen, 'Tokugawa and Modern Japan', in *Studies in Institutional History of Early Modern Japan*, ed. by J.W. Hall (Princeton: Princeton University Press, 1968), pp. 325-8; also Ronald P. Dore, *Education in Tokugawa Japan* (London: Routledge & Kegan Paul, 1965).
20. Lehmann, *Roots of Modern Japan*, pp. 121-8.
21. John C. Roberts, *Mitsui* (New York: Waterhill, 1973), p. 7; Olando D. Russell, *The House of Mitsui* (Westport: Greenwood Press, 1939); J. Hirschmeier and Yui, *Development of Japanese Business* . . . , pp. 57-66.

CHAPTER III

Pre-British India: A Hostile Climate

INDIA PERHAPS was much better off economically than the small island country when the Tokugawas established their hegemony in Japan. Commercial revolution was already under way and we come across the names of a number of big merchants who possessed enormous liquid capital, traded on an extensive scale, and dealt in goods of various descriptions. The Gujarat region with its locational advantages naturally had a lion's share of these commercial tycoons—Virji Vora, Hari Vaishya and Harji Parekh at Surat, Shantidas Zaveri, Surjit Naik and Kapurchand Bhansali at Ahmedabad to mention only a few—but they operated in other regions as well, such as Malaya, Kasi Viranna Narsimha Ramachetti and Ratanswamy Mudaliyar in different ports of south India, and a number of Jain merchants in eastern India. Their position in their respective regions was unassailable and neither the Indian rulers, nor the foreign traders, not to speak of the common people, could easily dispense with their services and help. In business power and resources. Japan in the seventeenth and the eighteenth centuries had few or none to compare with these merchant princes.[1]

India also had many more large urban centres such as Delhi, Agra, Lahore, Amritsar, Ahmedabad, Surat, Cambay, Pulicat, Masalipatnam, Murshidabad and Patna, to mention only the most populous among them. Its commercial intercourse with other parts of the world was also growing and received a further boost as a result of the expanding presence of the European East India Companies which started operating in the Indian market around AD 1600. Little of what they could bring from their home countries held much interest for the Indian consumer. They were mainly interested in procuring cargo from India. Indian products, particularly textiles, indigo, saltpetre and spices, were in great demand in European countries. For instance, so popular was the Indian calico that the British government had to revise its custom regulations twice within a short span of 20 years—once in 1700 and then in 1720—to discourage the inflow of Indian textiles.[2]

While collecting cargo from India, however, the European companies did not keep in mind only the home markets; for merely bilateral trade would have been hardly sufficient to sustain their operations. They also picked up products which were in demand in other countries. Thus developed a system of triangular trade. To sustain their complicated operations, the European trading companies quite frequently had to borrow money from Indian merchants, often at exorbitant rates of interest. All this testifies to the fact that the balance of trade must have been in favour of India.[3] In the absence of precise statistics, it is not easy to determine when India began to lose ground but perhaps the process of reversal started around the middle of the eighteenth century. The British occupation of Bengal in 1757 which set them on an imperial course boosted the position of the English East India Company precisely when the industrial revolution, which had just begun in Great Britain, was opening up the Indian markets for the import of cheaper machine-made textiles.

A large portion of the gains accruing to India in these favourable times went to the mercantile classes. As the artisans and craftsmen—the primary producers of most Indian goods in demand abroad—were too poor to finance their operations, they had to depend on merchants for the capital. The merchants advanced the required amount not as loan but a sort of earnest money for the intended output, the price of which would be fixed at the time of advancing the money. The price so fixed usually favoured the merchant because the other party had very little bargaining power. This so-called putting out system was, thus, heavily weighted against the primary producer; it was to the merchant that all the profits, went whether it resulted from upward price fluctuations, or from export, or even from inland trade. We have Bernier's testimony in support: 'If money be gained, it does not in any measure go into his [artisan's] pocket, but only serves to increase the wealth of the merchant.'[4] The fate of the weaver, who manufactured textile goods in which the Europeans were mainly interested, was no better. Poverty remained his constant companion.

The mercantile communities used their gains to finance their traditional activities, viz., trade and moneylending. Our knowledge of the economic activities and institutions of this period is still rather scanty, but whatever little we know suggests that neither in its basic character nor in its functional aspects did Indian business undergo substantial qualitative change. Neither the merchant princes nor their brethren down the line with lesser resources did anything to advance the frontiers of economic activities. The result was that even though some feeble signs of a commercial revolution was visible in India around the turn of the seventeenth century, it failed to gain momentum and consolidate itself during the next two hundred years. And this despite the fact that after the collapse of the Mughal empire in the first quarter of the eighteenth century, the dependence of the political power on the merchant princes had increased substantially in almost every part of the country.

A large majority of the Indian merchants of this period were Hindus. Most of them belonged by and large to the Vaishya group of castes or to the communities conventionally associated with the business profession. Muslims pursuing business career were much fewer in number and most of them traced their descent from the Hindu mercantile castes and communities. The Khojas, Bohras and Memons for instance—the three most important Muslim groups active in business in Gujarat—were converts from Hindu merchant castes and still retain, as a hangover of the past, some of their pre-conversion business practices even though these might conflict with Islamic injunctions. The Parsees, later to emerge so prominent on the Indian business horizon, were still engaged primarily in agricultural pursuits or petty trade in the countryside of Gujarat.[5] The social composition of a very large segment of Indian business, thus, was by and large in conformity with the occupational division envisioned in the *Varnashrama* scheme. In other words, the persons belonging to castes and communities, other than the ones identified with business by long social sanction, remained more or less aloof from commercial pursuits. True, we do find stray instances of a few Brahmans and Rajputs indulging in banking and trading, particularly in Gujarat, but these were exceptions to the general pattern rather than indicative of the trend.[6]

On the face of it, this seems to substantiate the position of the cultural determinist, who attributes the slow transformation of Indian business to the allegedly non-materialist character of

Hinduism. Apart from the theoretical difficulties, outlined in an earlier chapter and the fact that Hinduism, like all major religions of the world, places equal stress on material and non-material sides of life,[7] available empirical evidence about the behaviour of Indian businessmen during this period militate against such a proposition. The ruthless business practices of the Jain Virji Vora and Shantidas Zaveri or the Hindu traders in south India or the Muslim merchants of Surat would find little support in their religious prescriptions. A number of European travellers, who visited India at this time, felt that the Indian merchants were as shrewd as the devil, and that they were nowhere behind their Western counterparts in business acumen and judgement.[8]

True, the mercantile interests, like the rest of Indian society, clung to religious rituals in their personal lives, but as far as their business practices and activities were concerned, they deviated considerably from the spirit of their faiths or reinterpreted it to justify the deviations as legitimate. In other words, there was a wide gap between the normative precepts and actual practices.[9] Thus, if the business behaviour of the mercantile interests did not exhibit a great deal of creativity, and the non-mercantile communities, by and large, remained confined to the occupational boundaries imposed by the caste system and sanctified by the scriptures as well as tradition, the explanation must lie not so much in the religious and cultural constraints as in some other factor or set of factors.

II

A clue to the understanding of this phenomenon lies in the climate for enterprise prevailing in India almost up to the end of the eighteenth century. It kept the size of the market limited and offered little stimulus for business expansion and creativity on one hand and occupational mobility on the other. To elucidate this observation, let us review various aspects of the Indian situation in the seventeenth and the eighteenth centuries—the period during which the Japanese climate was becoming increasingly more favourable for industrial change.

To look at the political condition. Although the fissiparous forces—a variety of races, religions, cultures and languages coupled with the continental dimension of the country—have always been much stronger than the forces of unity in Indian history, India at the turn of the sixteenth century was much better identifiable as a distinct territorial entity than Japan. Thanks to the commitment to a common, though elusive, heritage and the exploits of some great monarchs, who held away over a large part of the country at different points of Indian history—Ashoka, Samudragupta, Allauddin Khalji and Muhammad Tughlaq to mention the most prominent among them—India was less of a mere geographical expression than Japan which had never experienced political unity before the Tokugawas. However these imperial unities survived for relatively short periods and remained too fragile to create substantial impact on the economy.[10]

The partial reunification achieved by Akbar a few decades before the Tokugawas brought Japan under their undisputed control, suffered the same fate as the imperial unities under the Maurya, Gupta, Khalji and Tughlaq kings. Neither Akbar nor his two successors ruled over the entire country and Aurangzeb, whose sway extended over practically the whole of the subcontinent, remained too preoccupied with a continuing series of warfare and internal revolts to stabilize his power, with the result that the territorial unification effected by him was torn to pieces almost on the morrow of his death. In other words, the process of unification which started with Akbar was aborted before it became an enduring reality, capable of creating a multiplier effect on economic and business activities. And yet, the Mughal century did witness some boost in commercial activities, largely due to the administrative integration of the maritime region of Gujarat and Bengal with the rest of the subcontinent.

The relations between the Great Mughals and the merchants remained, on the whole cordial but distant. Land revenue, transit duties, custom collection and a variety of cesses, imposts and tributes yielded more than sufficient income to meet the financial needs of the empire, and a well organized revenue administration ensured proper and timely collection of the taxes. The Mughals in their heyday, thus, did not need the merchant to help the state financially or in revenue collection, although most of the Mughal emperors tried to keep the influential sections of the mercantile community in good humour. It is significant that not only Akbar and his two successors but also Aurangzeb, despite his fanatical attitude to religion, avoided hurting the religious sentiments of the powerful Jain business community.[11] Nevertheless, no businessman, howsoever powerful, could dictate terms or pressurize the emperor or the imperial bureaucracy.

In contrast, the large number of successor regimes that emerged on the ruins of the Mughal empire following Aurangzeb's death in 1707 could hardly function without the support and help of the merchants. The small principalities into which the subcontinent was divided could seldom manage their affairs with the money collected from their subjects in taxes, and with their meagre resources were not in position to organize an efficient revenue collection machinery. Under these conditions, they found it expedient to farm out the revenue collection to principal merchants in their respective territories, and the merchants in turn provided much needed finances to carry on administration or military operations. The merchants were useful in another way: they could transmit large sums of money through their elaborate, countrywide network of ***hundi*** transaction. No other instrumentality could have been as effective and as safe in the grievously dismembered polity of post-Aurangzeb India. As the imperial treasury system, utilized for imperial money transfer in earlier days, ceased to function, the nobles and the officers of the empire, and even the emperor himself, had to rely upon the services of the merchant for this purpose. In fact, there was hardly any state or principality in the subcontinent which could function without the help of the merchant. Never in its long history had India witnessed such a close political-commercial nexus, investing the mercantile interests with enormous clout and influence.[12]

A few examples will suffice to illustrate this point. In Banaras, which emerged virtually as an independent kingdom by the middle of the eighteenth century, the banking house of Gopaldas Manohardas played the most critical role in the financial transactions of the state. The house of Kashmiri Mal, as the official bankers of the nawab of Awadh, provided financial and diplomatic guarantee for his obligations to the East India Company. The bankers, particularly the house of Pestonjee Merjee, had come to occupy a pivotal position in the financial management of the Nizam's territories even before Hyderabad became virtually independent of Mughal authority. The house of Hari Bhaktis, operating from Poona as well as from Baroda, provided financial accommodation to the Peshwas and the Gaikwads, and acted as a financial link between the various constituents of the Maratha confederacy. Another banker who operated in the Maratha kingdom during Bajirao Peshwa II (1796-1818) was Khusroshet Modi. And in Bengal at the other end of the country, Jagat Seth, Omi Chand and Khwaja Wazid were among the most important merchants who managed the finances of the province under the nawab.[13] To elaborate our argument we would describe in some greater details the way two of these banking houses operated in their respective regions—one in the west and the other in the east.

The house of Hari Bhaktis took its name from two brothers—Hari and Bhakti—whose family originally belonged to a small village near Baroda. When and how they left their village and grew very rich belongs to the realm of legend and speculation. What is certain is that for some time they operated from Poona, the capital of the Peshwas, providing a variety of financial services to the Maratha rulers. Later when Baroda emerged as an independent state in the last quarter of the eighteenth century under the Gaekwads, albeit still owing nominal allegiance to the Poona court, the Gaekwad capital became the main theatre of the Hari Bhaktis' operations. They were the most important of the five banking houses which acted as the *potedars* to the state. In this capacity, they provided finances to the state to meet its administrative expenses. In return they had the claim on the revenue of specified territories. The *modus operandi* was simple. Whenever the government required money, it would issue a warrant to the *potedar*. Accompanying the warrant would be a letter of credit ordering the rent collector of some territory to reimburse the *potedar* from the revenue still to be collected. Sometimes the *potedar* also paid directly to those who had claims against the state. The house, thus, acted as some sort of a bank to the state. In this fashion, the state could dispense with the need to have an elaborate revenue administration or an efficient treasury without unduly worrying about the resources to manage its affairs. As bankers, the Hari Bhaktis must have found the system quite beneficial as seldom, if ever, were the financial transactions between them and the state audited.[14]

In comparison to the Hari Bhaktis, the Jagat Seths were incredibly more rich and infinitely more influential. In fact, none of the Indian bankers of the eighteenth century could boast of as much power and pelf. Unlike the Hari Bahktis, they were not the sons of the soil of Bengal which was the theatre of their action.

Their forefathers had come from far off Rajasthan (Nagaur in the Marwar region) without any resources and amassed some wealth through moneylending and trading. By the time Bengal emerged as an autonomous region under the nawab, all but independent of the Mughal court, the Seths had already carved out a distinct enough place for themselves among the merchants of the region to deserve the title of Jagat Seth from Emperor Farrukhsiyar (1713-19). Nawab Murshid Quli Khan (1701-26) had them appointed as the treasurer general of Bengal in which capacity the Seths held the keys to the treasury, made payments against the warrant drawn by the government and received money on its behalf. They also stood as a security for the regular and timely payment of land revenue by the zamindars and controlled the mint. Their position became still stronger during the reigns of Murshid Quli's successors with the result that they became the lynchpin in the economic and political management of the suba. It is well known that the English victory at Plassey, marking the beginning of the British rule in India, was largely due to their support.[15]

Despite all their wealth and influence, however, the primary area of the Jagat Seth's business exploits remained the province of Bengal. Merchant princes operating in other parts of the country, too, remained confined by and large to their respective regions. Had they looked upon the entire subcontinent as the possible source of business opportunities, they could have used their position and financial clout to advance the course of capitalism, but they operated by and large at the local and regional levels. Perhaps the political jurisdictions of the princes they were so closely aligned with acted as a severe check on the expansion of their operations. Their commercial interactions with other regions were as restricted as the political contact or cooperation among their political mentors. All this goes to suggest that the commercial integration of the country which started during Akbar's reign received a major setback following the disintegration of the Mughal empire.

Conceivably, political fragmentation in itself should not have been sufficient to constrict the expansion of business and commerce. For, political unity cannot be regarded as the sole or even the most important factor in economic and business growth. Many instances can be cited of societies witnessing industrial breakthroughs even without political unification—Western Europe, particularly Germany, providing a most glaring illustration. In the case of pre-nineteenth century India, however, there were several other factors which reinforced the ill-effects of territorial dismemberment—or of a fragile and transient political unity at best. The lack of an effective transport system was one of these. The pre-British rulers did build a few roads but they were grossly inadequate for a country of continental dimensions. The Report of the Famine Commission of 1880 observed with only slight exaggeration that before the British rule, there existed 'not a single road . . . worthy of name'.[16]

Movement of goods and people, thus, was never very secure but conditions became far worse during the later Mughals, partly as a result of frequent Maratha raids mostly in western and central India, and the rise of highly organized brigand groups like the Thugs and the Pindaris. So seriously was the transport system neglected by successive rulers that even as late as in the middle of the nineteenth century, most regions of the country had no roads worth the name, and the country tracks were not good enough even for bullock carts—the quickest means of transport available then.[17] Referring to the Bombay Presidency, a perceptive observer pointed out in the early 1860s that the bullockcarts and pack bullocks carrying the produce of Berar took about two months to cover a distance of about 500 miles to Bombay city and in this process the consignment was exposed to rain, dirt and dust and 'to every species of depreciation'.[18] Conditions were similar if not worse in other parts of the country.

Another disincentive to movement was the existence of an intricate network of custom barriers—or *chowkies* as they were called in popular parlance. Having existed at least since the Mauryan times, these barriers had multiplied manifold largely on account of repeated political fragmentation. So deeply was the system entrenched that even the rise of the Mughals made little dent on it. Understandably, goods passing from the territories of one ruler to those of another were subject to custom clearance; cesses, however, were collected at multiple points even if the consignment transited within the jurisdiction of a single ruler or chieftain. The *chowkies* continued to exist throughout the Mughal empire even in its heyday, and the collection points increased rather than decreased with the weakening of the empire. On the basis of available evidences, it would be fair to suggest that almost anyone who could assert a measure of administrative authority—be it a provincial ruler, local chieftain, or a powerful zamindar, or in many cases all of them—could exact payment on goods passing through their territories. Thevenot, who visited India in the first quarter of the eighteenth century, counted sixteen custom points within a distance of less than 60 miles.[19]

The extensive and intricate web of custom barriers not only increased the duration of transit but also added to the cost of transport—and thus inflated the price of the commodity. According to a contemporary observer, 'between the time of leaving the factory or port and reaching their destination, goods and merchandise pay double their cost price in tolls'[20] The harassing and corrupt behaviour of the custom officials made the conditions still more exasperating. The possible impact of all this has been graphically described by Moreland in the following words:

> In the circumstances it is not possible to define the burden on commerce in quantitative terms, since any one might claim a tax of any amount, even if goods had paid taxes in an adjoining jurisdiction. Some of the charges of which were in themselves moderate, while others were apparently excessive. In one case, we read of a charge of two rupees per cent, in another of 65 rupees, and payments clearly varied within wide limits; but the real evil consisted in the uncertainty of the demand and the violence with which it was collected. Merchants could not make a confident forecast of what they would have to pay on any particular journey, and goods would not be transported unless the anticipated profit was sufficiently large to leave a margin of unforessen demands; in the long run the consumer doubtless paid the duties which were actually levied, but consumers and producers alike must have suffered by the curtailment of trade resulting from the uncertainty in the operation of the system.[21]

A plethora of currencies circulating in different part of the country was yet another factor the merchants had to contend with. The barter system, though still prevalent extensively, was already losing ground even before the beginning of the Mughal empire, thanks to the issuance of a large number of coins by the previous rulers in different parts of India. And it is now a well accepted fact that the Indian economy was fairly monetized by the end of Akbar's reign.[22] The monetization process continued to gain momentum during the successive Mughal rulers. The currencies issued by the previous regimes, however, did not disappear altogether and continued to circulate along with the Mughal coins.

As the empire disintegrated, local chiefs in various regions of India struck their own coins which swelled the ranks of currencies already circulating in different parts of the country—Mahmudi in Gujarat, Mughal rupees in northern India, Pagodas in the south being among the most important. That almost a thousand types of currencies were in circulation in India as late as in the end of the eighteenth century amply reflects the ill-effect of frequent territorial fragmentation of the land on one of the most critical business instrumentalities.[23]

Some of these currencies depreciated in value with the passage of time, and in the absence of an effective and established system of exchange, the *sahukars* and moneylenders fixed their own arbitrary rates. Under these conditions even the *hundi* system, perfected by the Indian *sahukars* to remit large sums over long distances, would have offered little protection against the problems created by a multiplicity of currencies. The remittance charges at any rate must have been very high. The situation was hardly favourable for the growth of inter-regional trade.

Weights and measurers presented a still more chaotic picture. Standards varied not only between region and region, province and province, or district and district but sometimes even between two neighbouring villages. For instance, *seer*, a basic unit of weight used all over the country, ranged in value between 20.62 *tolas* and 78 *tolas* in different parts of Bellary district (now in Karnataka) whereas in the neighbouring district of Dharwar the range was between 20 and 116 *tolas*. In Malda (Bengal) a seer was equal to as many as sixteen different values ranging between 50 and 105 *tolas*—while in Cuttack (Orissa) it ranged between 26 and 150 *tolas*. That is not all. The same basic unit of weight would have different values for different articles. In Azamgarh district (Utter Pradesh), for instance an 80-*tola* seer was used for weighing cotton while for ghee and salt it would be of 95 *tola* and for corn of 105 *tola*. Even the standards for buying and selling varied at some places. Referring to this confusing situation, a nineteenth-century writer has observed: 'It is as if some old manufacturer had made hundreds of weights and vessels of all different sizes, and then dropped them promiscuously from a balloon, each to be adopted by the inhabitants of the district, where it fell, as their standard.' The state of measures was no less complex. For instance, *gaz* (as basic measuring unit) would vary in length, depending on the kind of cloth being sold.[24] The hangover of the use of a bewildering variety of weights and measures persisted in some parts of India until much after independence.

As a logical consequence of these politico-economic factors India remained a congeries of regional markets—each limited to two to three hundred miles. Only in the areas connected by sea or where water routes were available were the markets somewhat more integrated. While the specialized products such as indigo, saltpetre and textiles commanded markets of somewhat larger sizes, most of the consumer goods—particularly foodgrains, which perished faster and therefore involved relatively heavier transport cost—moved within very limited areas. This, among other things, was the primary factor that continued to sustain the village self-sufficient economy of India. Whatever the other virtues of the economy based on self-sufficient villages or by and large segregated markets, it could not have been conducive to the growth of large-scale commercial activities.

Then, business operations even in these limited markets had to contend very often with unpredictable and arbitrary interference of political authorities. Since far flung regions could not be governed from the imperial capital, the provincial governors were left relatively free in matters of administration. Some of them indulged in commercial pursuits themselves and had no qualms in using their political position to futher their personal business interests at the cost of the ordinary merchants, even if the central authorities, particularly the emperor, would be more favourably disposed towards the mercantile classes. Several cases of the Mughal provincial governors declaring personal monopoly over the trade of certain profitable commodities without prior notice are recorded in documentary materials. A Jaunpur-based Jain merchant of the seventeenth century, Banarasidas, has in his autobiography provided a graphic account of how he and his associates were subjected to nerve-wrecking harassment by the local authorities simply because they could not meet the governor's demand for an unusually large sum. We also have the contrasting picture of the Sultans of Golconda and Bijapur providing facilities and encouragement to businessmen in their territories.[25] What emerges from these conflicting evidences is the fact that all depended on the personal whims and caprices of the local authorities, and the merchants even during the high noon of the empire were not quite sure of how they would be treated, when the attitude towards them would change for the better or for the worse, or what facilities or impediments their operation would have to contend with. Conditions became still worse during the twilight years of the empire.

While these constraints placed a limit on investment opportunities as well as on the will to invest, the taxation policy of the times adversely affected the generation of investible capital. Our knowledge of the taxation system under the pre-Mughal rulers is not very authentic, but it is inconceivable that the new rulers attempted a sharp break from the earlier practices. The major source of imperial income under the Mughals was the land revenue, custom duties on imports and exports, charges on the farming of the mint, inheritance tax and the presents the emperor claimed on several occasions. The land revenue charged in various forms amounted to nearly half the gross produce of the soil.[26] This in itself would have been sufficient to hamper savings even if we ignore the impact of other three major sources of imperial revenue, rates of which were usually high.

In addition to imperial taxes, various kinds of impost were charged by local authorities. According to Jadunath Sarkar these were at least fifty-four in number during Aurangzeb's reign. To substantiate the view that practically none escaped the extensive taxnet of the local authorities, Sarkar quotes from contemporary accounts:

> On the road and ferries . . . no rider was allowed to go on unless he paid a *dinar* and no pedesrian unless he paid a *dirham*. On the river highways, if the wind brought it to the ears of the toll collectors that the stream was carrying away a broken boat without *hasil* [revenue], they would chain the river. . . . They considered it an act of unparalleled leniency if no higher *zakat* [toll tax] was taken from rotten clothes actually worn than from mended rags, and a deed of extreme graciousness if cooked food was charged with a duty lower than uncooked grains. None of the Delhi sovereigns, in spite of their efforts to strengthen the faith and follow the rules of the Prophet, put down these illegal practices, but connived at them.[27]

Obviously, an exaggerated, rhetorical account, but still suggestive of the actual state of affairs. And if this was the situation under the Great Mughals, what came to prevail in later times can be anybody's guess.

Added to the high rate of taxation was the opressiveness built into the collection machinery. Land revenue which in a predominantly agricultural economy naturally formed the bulk of the total demand in taxes was collected through intermediaries. During the heyday of the empire the jagirdars or zamindars were expected to collect from the cultivator a stipulated amount, but in actual practice they always exacted much more as there was practically no check on their authority. With the entry of the merchant princes into the system in later years, guaranteeing the zamindar's commitment or claiming the revenue of specified areas in exchange for financial assistance extended to the state; the collection machinery became still more oppressive. In actual practice, thus, the incidence of taxation must have been much higher than fixed in law. In fact, it is reasonable to believe that a large part of the agricultural surplus, if not the whole of it, was extracted in revenue.

This must have sapped the cultivator's will and ability to invest in improving his operations. According to a contemporary observer, the land was 'seldom tilled, otherwise than by compulsion' and the cattle used to carry on agriculture was of poor breed.[28] As for the farming technology, Buchanan, writing at the turn of the nineteenth century, has given the following description of the implements and techniques used near Seringapatanam:

> Ameliorating succession of crops is utterly unknown, scarcely any attention is paid to the improvement of the breed of cattle, and still less to providing them with sufficient nourishment. . . . Owing to the extreme imperfection of their implements, and want of strength in their cattle, a field after six or eight ploughings, has numerous small bushes remaining as upright in it as before labour commenced; while the plough has not penetrated above three inches deep and has turned over no part of the soil. . . . The plough . . . has neither coulter nor mould board, to divide, and to turn over the soil; and the handle gives the ploughman very little power to command its direction. The other instruments are equally imperfect. . . .[29]

The situation in the rest of the country was more or less similar with only minor variations. Writing a few decades after Buchanan, an American consular officer in India observed that the Indians were carrying on their agricultural activities in almost the same fashion as at the time of Alexander's invasion of their country![30]

It is no surprise under these conditions that the farm sector experienced practically no change, quantitatively or qualitatively. The area under cultivation expanded only marginally during the seventeenth and the eighteenth centuries and foodgrains continued to form the bulk of agricultural produce. Even though there was some increase in the acreage of indigo and sugarcane in India during Jehangir's reign, commercialization of agriculture made little headway. In fact, the first feeble steps towards raising commercial crops would not be taken until the middle of the nineteenth century. Because of all these factors, agriculture provided for nothing more than bare subsistence to the actual producer, high yield per acre notwithstanding.

Theoretically, business expansion is possible alongside high rate of taxation or appropriation of agricultural surplus provided the amount extracted is invested in productive purposes. Efficient use of resources, however, was a virtue neither the Mughal state nor the successor regimes could boast of. In the words of a competent authority, 'a cavalier indifference to economy characterized every branch of the administration and the army'[31] under the Mughals. Conspicuous display of imperial grandeur, palace luxuries, and internecine warfare claimed a preponderantly larger share of the money spent than activities which could produce a multiplier effect on the economy.

Viewed collectively, these material contents in the constellation of forces were incapable of inducing new, easily perceivable opportunities for profit at a scale that could have lured new entrants into business, abandoning the occupations their forefathers had pursued for a long time. The ideational aspects of the constellation were no less inhibitive of occupational mobility. Education is regarded as one of the most critical elements in moulding the economic behaviour of a people. And in India a large section of the population was either uneducated or the product of institutions run or controlled by religions establishments—*pathashalas* in case of Hindus, *maqatabs* or *madarasas* in case of Muslims, and similar outfits for other numerically less populous groups. The curriculum, content, and method of teaching in these institutions were such that served to reinforce, instead of acting as a liberating influence, religious dogmas, rituals, and prescriptions. Commenting on the Hindu educational system around the tenth century AD. Al-Beruni averred that it kept the pupil ignorant of the outer world and of the arts and sciences of the West. The situation was not very different eight hundred years later, as several authorities have testified.[32] In practically all cases, the Indian educational system well up to the end of the eighteenth century was largely confined to the learning of classics, languages, literature and scriptures.

This kind of education coupled with stagnation in business opportunities helped to sustain the occupational structure propped up by the caste systems and long social sanction among the Hindus; persons belonging to other communities too seldom deviated from the callings they had come to be associated with. Worse still, it precluded any worthwhile technical and scientific advancement. Much has been written about the Indian contribution to science and technology in ancient and medieval times and we can still see the evidences of outstanding feats in these respects in many parts of the country. That the Indian artisans and craftsmen could produce goods involving great manual dexterity—Dacca muslins and Patan saris are oft-quoted examples—also cannot be denied. However, the scientific knowledge and craftsmanship possessed by the Indians did not have a multiplier effect because little attention was paid to develop appropriate tools of enquiry—experimental techniques, equipments or apparatus required for it—or maintain institutions engaged in sustained search for new skills. As the educational curriculum remained heavily weighted in favour of languages and classics, applied skills were passed on from father to son generation after generation. All this was bound to result in routinisation of certain skills instead of encouraging enquiry and experimentation which widespread illiteracy futher enforced. Such a society could hardly develop a strong technological tradition or sustain it for a long time. There is a general consensus that whatever might have been the situation in the earlier times. Indian technological genius had exhausted itself much before the colonization process of the country began.[33] Buchanan's observation that 'in India it is seldom that an attempt is made to accomplish anything by machinery that can be performed by human labour' is an accurate description of the technological temper of the Indian society. It is no surprise, therefore, that 'a relatively stagnant technology and rather rudimentary implements were characteristic features of manufacturing' as was the case with agriculture.[34] Worse still, urge and competence to develop new and improved devices were almost non-existent.

On the top of this all, the low esteem in which business was held in the society must have been yet another disincentive to pursuing a business career. Long long ago, Kautilya had asserted that the businessman was essentially a thief although he was not expressly called so. Whether the image of the profession in later periods improved, as is suggested by some authorities, is debatable, but there is general agreement that during the medieval times, businessman did not enjoy very high social status, partly because of the unscrupulousness, greed, and grubbiness associated with him in the popular mind. If Abul Fazl found that 'honesty and conscientiousness are rare' among businessmen of his times, a nineteenth-century Rajasthani proverb—'the Jain *bania* insists on filtering water before drinking it, but has no compunction in drinking (sucking) the blood of the poor unfiltered' (meaning relentless exploitation)—echoed a similar feeling four centuries later. Profit motive and those engaged in profit-making are generally suspect in a relatively poor society, and the attitude of the Mughal ruling class, which had no particular use for the businessman, could not have helped upgrade his social image.[35]

This is a rather generalized account of the material environment in India in pre-British India, shaping the motivation and activities of its people. Admittedly, the state of a society over such a long span of time cannot be compressed in a few paragraphs and any generalization about such a complex society as India will probably be an oversimplification. Regional variation undoubtedly did exist and it is not suggested that all these factors affected every part of India in equal measure. This caveat notwithstanding, the conditions described above would roughly approximate the climate which influenced the business behaviour in India almost up to the rise of the British power in the country.

It is obvious that the climate was not very favourable. It will be agreed that a weak economic infrastructure, like the one prevailing in pre-1800 India, was incapable of offering any meaningful induce-ment to those already in business for making a major departure from their age-old proven practices. Also, it could not have pointed to definite opportunity gain to non-commercial classes if they were to give up their traditional professions in favour of business. Probably it would be fair to maintain that the mercantile castes and communities, having pre-empted the limited business opportunities perceivable under the conditions prevailing then, did not leave much room for others to aspire for business careers. As D.R. Gadgil has rightly pointed out 'in Hindu society there was no mobility between the merchant trader classes and the military-priestly, and ruling administrative classes'. According to another authority, whatever little social and occupational mobility the Hindu society experienced, it 'occurred within an essentially stable, relatively unchanging system'.[36] There is no evidence to suggest that the situation was any different among other sections of population.

Entrepreneurial response, as distinct from adventure or gambling, consists in moderate risk-taking engendered by a combination of achievement motivation and expectancy of reward.[37] A significantly qualitative change in the dynamics of Indian business under the conditions outlined above would have amounted to more than moderate risk as the environment was incapable of promising a high expectancy of reward. This more than anything else explains the static character of Indian business during this period. In other words, if there remained a rough equilibrium between the perceivable opportunities on one hand, and business behaviour and occupational division of the society on the other, it was because the prevailing constellation of forces would not permit a bolder, more creative response.

III

It was only around the beginning of the nineteenth century that this equilibrium began to be disturbed. Two principal factors seem to have influenced this development: (i) the commercial operations of Europeans in India, particularly the British who overpowered others, and (ii) the changes in the material environment wrought by the burgeoning British power which brought practically the whole country under its hegemony by 1820.

European companies to trade with India were established around the beginning of the seventeenth century. At the initial stages, however, their fields of operations and their contact with the native population were very much limited and their familiarity with the country was inadequate. Lack of purchasing power—as the outflow of bullion was discouraged by their governments and demand for European goods was not very high in India—plagued their operations. These conditions naturally hampered their ability to have a critical impact on the behaviour of Indian businessmen.

The situation, however, began to change with the British

occupation of Bengal around the middle of the eighteenth century and the subsequent expansion of British authority. For one thing, it facilitated, in gradual stages, the entry of free merchants into the Indian markets. These merchants traded on their own account under the license secured from the English East India Company which had a monopoly to trade with India under a royal charter. As a result of the victory at Plassey, the English company secured the right to trade without paying inland duties. Very often the Company servants misused the corporate privilege to advance their personal business interests. In many instances, the free merchants would purchase the permit—or ***dastak*** in local language—at exorbitant price and made fortunes through inland trade. The Company servants actively collaborated in this game and very often also traded on their own account. Although the privileged inland trade was abolished in 1767,[38] the forces it had set in motion continued to gain momentum.

This was a new factor in Indian business which became increasingly more visible with the expansion of the political influence of the alien power. The methods of the British trader were dubious, exploitative, and arbitrary, but there is no doubt that his business decisions were characterized by greater aggressiveness, drive and imagination than his Indian counterparts—thanks, perhaps, to a superior entrepreneurial vision imbibed from the environment in his home country reinforced by an invisible bond of racial affinity with the new class of rulers of India. John Forbes in Bombay and Thomas Parry in Madras were among the earliest of such enterprising free traders and the companies established by them still survive in some form or the other.[39]

Some of these traders were so successful as to feel encouraged to establish agency connections with respectable British firms based in London or other important business centres in Great Britain, or set up their own branches there. Thus came into being a number of agency houses in the presidency cities of Calcutta, Bombay and Madras in the last decades of the eighteenth century. By the end of the century, Calcutta could boast of at least twenty-nine agency houses—Palmer & Co., Alexander & Co., Gruttendan & Co., Colvin & Co., McKintosh & Co., Ferguson & Co., and Pickards & Co. being the most important among them. Forbes & Co., Bruce Fawcatt & Co., and John Leckie & Co. were the better known firms in Bombay, and Parry & Co. was the most visible in the Madras region. All of these were set up either by free merchants, such as William Fairlie, John Ferguson, John Palmer, John Forbes and Thomas Parry, or company servants-turned-businessmen. A few of these were originally engaged in inland trade but moved into agency business later primarily to facilitate remittances to England by Englishmen residing in India, while others started off as agency houses but took to trading later since agency business in itself would have yielded little profit. Whatever their origin, they continued to add new lines to their businesses such as European type banking and steamshipping, although trade remained the mainstay of their operations in practically all cases. The number of agency houses increased and their activities expanded after the British East India Company lost its monopoly of India trade under the Charter Act of 1813.[40]

The operations of the free merchants and agency houses opened up new vistas for business, pointing to new opportunities waiting for exploitation. They promoted and financed indigo plantation, invested in saltpetre works, participated in the risky business of coal mining, established leather manufacturing and sugar refining, and at least one Englishmen wrestled, though unsuccessfully, with the almost impossible task of steel-making.[41] The message of their operations could not have been lost on Indian merchants, some of whom had close business interactions with them.

The demonstration effect generated by the Indian enterprises of alien businessmen was reinforced by a number of salutary developments which took place because of the concern of the new rulers of India to consolidate their power in the country. Among these were the beginnings of secular education and the spread of European liberalism. Although a formal declaration introducing English education had to wait until 1835, the process of secularization had been initiated much earlier with the establishment of the Hindu College in Calcutta in 1817. By the end of the first quarter of the century, the impact of Western ideas and new education was already noticeable, particularly in Bengal which was the first to fall in the British lap. There are repeated references in contemporary Bengali periodicals to unconventional behaviour, flouting customs and traditions of English educated youth, much to the chagrin of guardians and parents. These, however, were aberrations. On a more positive plane, the spread of new education 'installed into the minds of Indians a spirit of rational enquiry into the basis of their religion and society'.[42]

This was the beginning of a process which would in the long run loosen the tight grip of religious ideas and practices and dogmas and superstitions on the Indian society. But even in the short run, the intervention of new education and contact with Western ideas caused the kind of convulsion in the social ethos which the birth of Brahmo Samaj epitomized in the cultural sphere.[43] In the economic field, the new spirit reflected itself in the non-commercial classes looking at commercial opportunities more sympathetically and meaningfully than before, although for those already engaged in business, the stimulus was not strong enough to cause deviation from the beaten but proven path.

Viewed in this light, the enterprising endeavours of Dwarkanath Tagore would appear to lie in the logic of history. He had great admiration for Western ideas and culture, and as a close friend of Raja Rammohun Roy was a pillar of the Brahmo Samaj movement, The Calcutta Unitarian Committee which he founded jointly with his illustrious friend became an important vehicle to spread the message of European liberalism. It has been said of him that 'for a Bengali of the early nineteenth century, he was a most unusual man . . . enormously sophisticated as demonstrated in his meticulous choice of Western wine, music and food'.[44] Though a Brahman, he defied the Hindu taboos including the injunction against crossing the seas. With great command over the English language, he had developed very close contact with British officials and businessmen in his province.

While Dwarkanath and his associates were busy changing the social landscape in Bengal, the agency houses in the province came to grief consequent upon a severe depression in England which swept off their British affiliates who were deeply steeped in speculation. Tagore, 'equal of any Englishman in business acumen',[45] proceeded to fill the vacuum. Jointly with William Carr, an erstwhile indigo planter, he founded the Tagore Carr Company to reap commercial benefit through the same kind of activities which had been handled by the defunct agency houses earlier. He established a European type bank, a steamship company, and a colliery in addition to a host of minor ventures. Tagore belonged to a big landlord family and it is possible that the permanent land settlement, introduced in Bengal in the closing decade of the eighteenth century, had improved his financial position, which encouraged him to risk his capital in fields the Indian mercantile interests had largely shunned heretofore.[46]

According to his biographer, Dwarkanath was the first high-caste Hindu to enter business. Another member of the Tagore family, Prasanna Kumar, was one of the directors of the Union Bank founded by Tagore. Another Brahman, Radha Madhab Banerjee also appears on the list. These, by no means, were the only high caste individuals to enter the demeaning world of business. Between 1834 and 1847, a host of partnership firms were established jointly by Bengalis and Englishmen—an entirely new occurrence on the Indian business horizon—of which Tagore Carr, Oswald Seal, and Rustomji Turner were more prominent.[47] Their promoters like Tagore were close to the British ideologically and culturally while the traditional mercantile classes, safe in their traditional lines and unaffected by new values and ideas refrained from entering more challenging fields. These Indo-British partnerships disappeared from the scene around 1847, but this does not detract from the fact that they signified a breakthrough in Indian entrepreneurial pattern.

While these developments were effecting changes of far-reaching consequences in the business environment of eastern India, the embryo of a new managerial structure was gradually and imperceptibly taking shape. The origin of the managing agency system, as it would come to be known in its fully developed form, is shrouded in mystery. According to the most popular view, its roots lay in the concern of the British promoters of business enterprises in India to ensure efficient management of their Indian operations even after they retired to the more congenial climate at home. For this purpose, they would entrust their enterprises to the care of another expatriate businessman or firm for which the latter was suitably renumerated, most often through commission on earnings. In due course, the firm responsible for management would acquire sufficient financial stake in the enterprises it managed on behalf of their original promoters so that for all practical purposes the enterprises would become indistinguishable from the companies it directly controlled, though in theory it continued to be only a managing agent. According to another view, this kind of system was already prevalent in the older insurance companies.[48] Whatever its origin, it is fairly certain that the rudiments of the system were already known to the Calcutta business circles by the time the Tagore Carr Company was launched. For, this partnership firm became the nucleus of six different joint stock companies floated by Dwarkanath Tagore and his associates. Although many others contributed to the share capital of these companies, the authority to manage them remained with the Tagore Carr Company which jointly with its partners held the controlling shares in them. The company received for its labours a certain percentage of the earnings of the enterprises it managed.[49]

As there was no company law in India to limit the liability of the stock-holders, the number of companies organized as joint stocks naturally remained limited. Few followed Dwarkanath's lead to use a single enterprise as the nucleus to develop a conglomerate, comprising a number of units involved in a variety of business lines but remaining under a single managerial umbrella. The managing agency system thus did not come in general use immediately and in fact had to wait for another two decades before it would emerge as the universally accepted model for corporate management in India. But there is no doubt that its foundation had already been laid when the first ever company law was enacted in India in 1850.[50]

All these developments were still confined to Bengal. The regions which came under British occupation much later, where the demonstration effect of the business activities of agency houses and free merchants was still much less visible, and where neither the European liberal ideas nor reform movements had made much headway, remained practically unaffected by the kind of business propositions that had brought new entrepreneurs to the fore in Bengal. Strangely enough, even though western India could boast of a number of big merchants—Jamsedji Jejeebhoy Rustomji, Dadajee Dhackjee, Jagannath Shankarseth at Bombay and Hemabhai Vakhatchand, Hutheesing Kesrising and Maganbhai Karamchand at Ahmedabad to mention only a few at the two principal business centres in western India[51]—they like the Calcutta mercantile classes continued with their traditional business activities, viz., moneylending, trading, brokerage, commission agency, and in a few cases ship-building. If branching out into new lines would have meant opportunity loss to them, entering the demeaning world of business would have appeared quite risky, both socially and economically, to others. Western India under these conditions failed to produce a Dwarkanath Tagore or the Indo-British enterprises that straddled the Calcutta business horizon in the 1830s and 40s, despite substantial capital accumulation that had taken place thanks to the region's long involvement in inland trade and foreign commerce. Conditions in south and north India, where mercantile operations were still in general at a much more modest scale, were still worse.

Even the Bengali Indo-British enterprises remained confined to the lines of business opened up by the agency houses or free merchants. More unfamiliar and therefore riskier fields did not hold attraction for them. Tea plantation is a case in point. When the English East India Company established tea gardens in Assam in the early 1830s, following a decade-long search for tea plants in the hills, it did so with the declared intention to transfer the gardens to private enterprise once the experiment had demonstrated the capability of India to produce tea. By 1837, the company was ready to redeem its promise, but even the new breed of Bengali entrepreneurs, not to speak of the old-fashioned traders, showed little enthusiasm to avail of the opportunity. Dwarkanath Tagore and a few of his associates did make some half hearted attempts to form the Bengal Tea Association, but uncertain about the future they gladly stepped aside when a group of Englishmen decided to establish the Assam Company in 1838 in far off London. It was, thus, left to this British firm, whose determination survived a string of frustrations and colossal losses spanning over almost two decades, to prove the viability of an industry with such great prospects for the Indian economy.[52]

This is not to suggest that the business environment remained entirely static. Far from it. With the consolidation of the British power, Indians throughout the subcontinent began to sense political unity and stability once again after a long time. The marauding elements like the Thugs and Pindaris were virtually exterminated by the end of the 1830s. The process of creating a unified currency for the entire country had already started with the declaration in 1835 that the company rupee would be the legal tender throughout India, although efforts to standardize weights and measures were less successful. European type banking had also made limited headway, and the irksome custom barriers had been finally abolished by 1846. While the decision to spread English education had been taken as early as 1835, definite move to introduce railways and modern postal services was already on by the middle of the nineteenth century. The British Parliament in the meantime had lifted the ban on the export of technology out of Britain in 1843, making it possible for the Indians to import British machines.

Also with the expansion of the empire, Western ideas and liberalism began to creep slowly into the entire country, and the questioning attitude towards religious and social dogmas which had played such a critical role in the rise of new entrepreneurs in Bengal had already touched western India by the middle of the 1840s. In the words of a well-regarded authority:

> With the growth of the British power, the old order weakened and the confidence of the Indians in their own culture diminished. Many were dazzled by the civilization of the West, which seemed to be better adopted for the acquisition of temporal power. A few were so enchanted by it that they took to Western culture with the enthusiasm of neophytes and endeavoured to westernise themselves completely: some became Christians. . . . Not so the great majority. . . . The classes educated in English did not, as a rule, give up their traditional ways of life and habits of mind, but used western learning for improving their own culture and adopting it to the new impulses created by contact with the West.[53]

The rise of the new spirit would soon manifest itself in a series of reform movements in the Bombay-Gujarat region.

The above survey makes it clear that even if the Indian business environment was somewhat more positive than the Japanese around AD 1600, this could not be sustained. In fact the environment became gradually worse, so that it is difficult not to agree with Moreland that by the middle of the eighteenth century the overall situation had so deteriorated as 'to reduce the reward of production to a point where it ceased to offer an adequate incentive'.[54] Signs of some improvement in the Indian business environment began to develop with the rise of British paramountcy around the end of the eighteenth century—thanks to the political-economic needs of the colonial masters but unintended by them. But at the time when the first textile mill was set up in India in the middle of the nineteenth century, marking the beginning of modern industries, the changes were still at a nascent stage. The constellation of forces was yet to become sufficiently conducive to the rapid progress of industrial entrepreneurship.

This was in sharp contrast to the situation at the time of the birth of the textile industry in Japan where the two and a half centuries of Tokugawa rule had already prepared the ground, although unintendedly and without any conscious design, capable of yielding a rich harvest. Japan, without question, embarked upon industrial experiment with a much greater advantage.

NOTES

1. For accounts of merchant princes see W.H. Moreland, *India from Akbar to Aurangzeb* (London: Macmillan, 1923), pp. 145-85; S. Bhattacharya, *The East India Company and the Economy of Bengal, 1704-1740* (London: Luzac & Co. 1954), pp. 108-10; B.G. Gokhale, *Surat in the 17th Century: A Study in Urban History of Modern India* (London: Curzon Press, 1979); idem, 'Ahmedabad in the 17th Century', *Journal of the Economic and Social History of the Orient,* Vol. 12, No. 2 (April 1969); Ashin Das Gupta, *Indian Merchants and the Decline of Surat c. 1700-1750* (Wiesbaden: Franz Steiner Verlag, 1979); Surendra Gopal, 'Jain Merchants in Eastern India under Great Mughals' in *Business Communities of India: A Historical Perspective,* ed. by Dwijendra Tripathi (New Delhi: Manohar, 1984), pp. 69-82; Vijaya Ramaswamy, *Textiles and Weavers in Medieval South India* (Delhi: Oxford University Press, 1985).
2. Urban centres have been discussed in D.R. Gadgil, *Origins of Modern Indian Business Class* (New York: Institute of Pacific Relations, 1959). For India's commercial power, see S.A. Khan, *The East India Trade in the 17th Century in Political and Economic Aspects* (Oxford: Oxford University Press, 1923); Bal Krishna, *Commercial Relations Between India and England* (Oxford: Oxford University Press, 1924); and C.J. Hamilton, *The Trade Relations between England and India* (Calcutta: Thacker Spink and Co., 1919).
3. Susil Chaudhari, *Trade and Commercial Organization in Bengal, 1650-1720* (Calcutta: Firma K.L. Mukhopadhyay, 1975); C.H. Philips, *The East India Company, 1784-1834* (Bombay: Oxford University Press, 1961).
4. Quoted in Moreland, *India . . .* , p. 200. For a contemporary account, see George Rogues, 'Of Trade and Traders in 17th Century

India', trans. and ed. by Indrani Ray, Occasional Paper No. 26 (Calcutta: Centre for Studies in Social Sciences, 1979, mimeo.).

5. S.A.I. Tirmizi, 'Muslim Merchants of Gujarat' in *Business Communities . . .* , ed. by Tripathi, pp. 59-68; Amalendu Guha, 'More About the Parsi Seths: Their Roots, Entrepreneurship and Comprador Role, 1650-1918', *Economic and Political Weekly*, Vol. 19, No. 3 (21 January 1984); Ashok V. Desai, 'The Origins of Parsi Enterprise', *Indian Economic and Social History Review*, Vol. 5, No. 4 (Dec. 1968).
6. For details see Dwijendra Tripathi and M. Mehta, 'Class Character of the Gujarati Business Community' in *Business Communities . . .* , ed. by Tripathi, pp. 151-72.
7. The goal of life, according to Hindu ethos, are *dharma* (virtue), *artha* (material well-being), *kama* (sensuous pleasure) and *moksha* (ultimate salvation).
8. For a general description of the methods of Indian businessmen and the opinion of European travellers about them see Moreland, *India . . .* , pp. 145-855; see also S. Arasarathnam, 'Indian Merchants and Their Trading Methods—*Circa* 1700', *Indian Economic and Social History Review*, Vol. 3, No. 1 (March 1966); Ashin Das Gupta, 'The Merchants of Surat, *c.* 1700-50' in *Elites in South Asia*, ed. by E. Leach and S.N. Mukherjee (Cambridge: Cambridge University Press, 1970).
9. This kind of contradiction was not peculiar to Indian merchants. The behaviour of businessmen in other parts of the world justifies the impression that their business methods do not necessarily conform to their religious values. John D. Rockefeller, for instance, in his personal life was a deeply religious man but utterly ruthless in his business dealings. Likewise, Andrew Carnegie, well-known for his charities, adopted dubious means in his dealings with the labour. Allan Nevins, *Study in Power: John D. Rockefeller, Industrialist and Philanthropist* (New York: Charles Scribner's & Sons, 1953); Burton J. Hendrick, *The Life of Andrew Carnegie* (London: William Heinemann, 1933).
10. Morris's phrase 'from chaos to chaos in three generations' may be too strong but his basic point that at no time in Indian history did political unity survive for more than a century or a century and a half over any large region is substantially correct. M.D. Morris, 'Towards a Reinterpretation of the 19th Century Indian Economic History', *Journal of Economic History*, Vol. 23, No. 4 (Dec. 1963), pp. 606-18; see also the symposium on Morris's thesis in *Indian Economic and Social History Review*, Vol. 5, No. 1 (March 1968) and Morris's reply in vol. 5. No. 4 (Dec. 1968).

11. Gopal, 'Jain Merchants . . .'; see also Dwijendra Tripathi, *The Dynamics of a Tradition: Kasturbhai Lalbhai and His Entrepreneurship* (New Delhi: Manohar, 1981), pp. 22-32.
12. G.S.L. Devra, 'The Mughals State and Indian Business', in *State and Business in India: A Historical Perspective*, ed. by Dwijendra Tripathi (New Delhi: Manohar, 1987), pp. 1-21; Lakshmi Subramanian and Rajat K. Ray, 'Merchants and Politics: From the Great Mughals to the East India Company' in *Business and Politics in India: A Historical Perspective*, ed. by Dwijendra Tripathi (New Delhi: Manohar, 1991), pp. 19-95.
13. Subramanian and Ray, 'Merchants and Politics . . . ; V.D. Divekar, 'The Emergence of an Indigenous Business Class in Maharashtra in the 18th Century', *Modern Asian Studies*, Vol. 16, No. 3 (Oct. 1982); Sanjay Subramanyan and C.A. Bayly, 'Portfolio Capitalists and the Political Economy of Early Modern India', *Indian Economic and Social History Review*, Vol. 25, No. 4 (Oct.-Dec. 1988); Om Prakash, *The Dutch East India Company and the Economy of Bengal 1630-1720* (Delhi: Oxford University Press, 1983).
14. Dwijendra Tripathi and Priti Misra, *Towards a New Frontier: History of the Bank of Baroda* (New Delhi: Manohar, 1985), pp. 19-25.
15. J.H. Little, *The House of Jagat Seth* (Calcutta: Calcutta Historical Society, 1967); see also Bhattacharya, *The East India Company . . .*, pp. 104-31.
16. Quoted in Tarashankar Banerjee, *Internal Market of India, 1834-1900* (Calcutta: Academic Publishers, 1966), p. 61.
17. For detailed description, ibid., pp. 60-75.
18. Walter R. Cassels, *Cotton, An Account of Its Culture in the Bombay Presidency* (Bombay: Government Press, 1862), p. 299; see also Dwijendra Tripathi, 'An Echo Beyond the Horizon: The Effect of the American Civil War on India', *Journal of Indian History: Golden Jubilee Volume*, ed. by T.K. Ravindran (Trivandrum: University of Kerala, 1973).
19. Moreland, *India . . .*, p. 288; see also Banerjee, *Internal Market . . .*, Chap. 1: Charles E. Trevelyan in his *Report Upon the Internal Customs and Tour Duties of the Bengal Residency*, submitted in 1934.
20. Quoted in Moreland, *India . . .*, p. 291.
21. Ibid., p. 289.
22. Tapan Raychaudhary, 'The Mughal Empire' in the *Cambridge Economic History of India*, Vol. I, ed. by Tapan Raychaudhary and Irfan Habib (Cambridge: Cambridge University Press, 1980), pp. 172-93.
23. K.N.S. Namboodiripad, *A Short History of Indian Currency* (Poona: Continental Prakashan, 1955), pp. 1-15; see also Moreland,

India . . . , pp. 329-33; Om Prakash, 'On Coinage in Mughal India', *Indian Economic and Social History Review*, Vol. 25, No. 4 (Dec. 1988).

24. C.F. Grover, *Indian Weights and Measures* (Bombay: Government Press, 1863), pp. 5-11; the quote is on p. 6. The *seer* (a common unit of weight) in use until very recently in the Gujarat bazaars, for instance, was half of the *seer* used in the northern parts of India.
25. Moreland, *India* . . . , pp. 146-8; for Banarasidas's travails see his *Ardha Kathanak*, ed. by Nathuram Premi (Bombay: Sanshodhita Sahityamala, 1957); S. Arasaratnam, 'India and Indian Ocean: The Seventeenth Century' in Ashin Das Gupta and M.N. Pearson (eds.), *India and the Indian Ocean, 1500-1800* (Calcutta: Oxford University Press, 1987), pp. 104-24.
26. From a discussion of the Mughal tax structure see D. Pant. *The Commercial Policy of the Mughals* (Bombay: D.B. Taraporewala & Sons, 1930). For the poverty of Indian masses see Tara Chand, *Society and the State in the Moghul Period* (New Delhi: Govt. of India Publications Division, 1961), pp. 43-72.
27. Jadunath Sarkar, *Lectures on Mughal Administration* (Calcutta: M.C. Sarkar & Sons, 1921), p. 120.
28. Raychaudhuri, 'The Mughal Empire . . .', pp. 172-93. The quote is from Bernier on p. 175.
29. Quoted in T. Raychaudhuri, 'The Mid-Eighteenth Century Background' in *The Cambridge Economic History of India*, Vol. II, ed. by Dharma Kumar (Cambridge: Cambridge University Press, 1982), p. 16.
30. Dwijendra Tripathi, 'The United States and India: Economic Links, 1860-1900', Ph.D. Dissertation (University of Wisconsin, 1963), p. 119.
31. Raychaudhuri 'The Mughal Empire . . .', p. 172.
32. R.C. Majumdar, 'English Education' in *History and Culture of the Indian People*, Vol. X, pt. II: *British Paramountcy and Indian Renaissance* ed. by R.C. Majumdar (Bombay: Bharatiya Vidya Bhavan, 1965), pp. 31-52; see also P.L. Rawat, *History of Indian Education* (Agra: Ram Prasad & Sons, 1968), pp. 80-110. For a comparative discussion of education in many Asian countries including India and Japan, see Don Adam, *Education and Modernization in Asia* (Reading, Mass.: Addison-Wesley, 1970).
33. For details see A. Rahman, *Intellectual Colonization: Science and Technology in East-West Rotations* (New Delhi: Vikas, 1983); pp. 25-52; A Rahman *et al.*, *Science and Technology in India* (New Delhi: Indian Council for Cultural Relations, 1973), pp. 1-23; S. Bhattacharya, 'Cultural and Social Constraints on Technological

Innovations and Development. Some Case Studies' in *Science, Technology and Culture*, ed. by Surajit Sinha (New Delhi: India, International Centre, 1970), pp. 44-72; Irfan Habib, 'Technology and Barriers to Social Change in Mughal India', *Indian Historical Review*, Vol. 5, Nos. 1-2 (July 1978-Jan. 1979), pp. 152-74.

34. Raychaudhuri, 'The Mid-Eighteenth Century Background', pp. 18-19.
35. S. Ambirajan, 'Changing Attitudes Towards Business in India'; pp. 1-18; Abul Fazl's quotation is from *Ain-i-Akbari*, trans. by H. Blockman (Delhi: Oriental Books Reprint Corporation, 1965). Vol. I, p. 233.
36. Gadgil, *Origins of the Modern Indian Business Class* . . . , p. 23; Bernard Barber, 'Social Mobility in Hindu India' in *Social Mobility in the Caste System in India* (The Hague: Mouton Publishers, 1968), pp. 32-3.
37. For a detailed discussion of this concept, see David C. McClleland, *The Achieving Society* (Princeton: Van Nostrand, 1961), Chap. 6.
38. S.B. Singh, *European Agency Houses in Bengal* (Calcutta: Firma K.L. Mukhopadhyaya & Co., 1966), pp. 1-16; see also Ian B. Watson, *Foundation for Empire: English Private Trade in India* (New Delhi: Vikas, 1980).
39. Hilton Brown, *Parrys of Madras* (Madras: Parry & Co., 1954); R.A. Wadia, *A Forgotten Friend of India: Sir Charles Forbes* (Baroda: Padmaja Publication, 1948).
40. Singh, *European Agency Houses* . . . , pp. 17-35.
41. D.H. Buchanan, *The Development of Capitalistic Enterprise in India* (New York: Macmillan Co., 1934), pp. 278-9.
42. R.C. Majumdar, 'Impact of Western Culture' in *History and Culture*, Vol. X, pt. II, . . . pp. 89-96. The quote is on p. 92.
43. David Kopf, *The Brahmo Samaj and the Shaping of the Modern Indian Mind* (Princeton: Princeton University Press, 1979).
44. Ibid., p. 162; for more details of Tagore's career, see Blair B. Kling, *Partner in Empire: Dwarkanath Tagore and the Age of Enterprise in Eastern India* (Berkeley: University of California Press, 1976).
45. Kopf, *The Brahmo Samaj* . . . , p. 162.
46. Kling, *Partner in Empire: Dwarkanath Tagore and the Age of Enterprise in Eastern India* (Berkeley: University of California Press, 1976), p. 44; see also James W. Furrell, *The Tagore Family: A Memoir* (Calcutta: T.C. Bose & Co., 1892); Kissory Chand Mitra, *Memoir of Dwarkanath Tagore* (Calcutta: Thacker Spink & Co., 1870).
47. N.K. Sinha, 'Sources and Problems of Business History in India in the First Half of the 19th Century' in *Proceedings of the 37th Session* (New Delhi: Indian Historical Records Commission, 1966); see also

N.K. Sinha, 'Indian Business Enterprise: Its Failure in Calcutta (1800-1848)', *Bengal Past and Present*, Diamond Jubilee Number (July-Dec. 1967).

48. The controversy about the origin of the managing agency system has not yet been resolved despite a host of works. While most writers trace it to the old British enterprises in general, Radhey Shyam Rungta suggests that the system originated with the early banking and insurance activities of the agency houses. For detailed discussions see P.S. Loknathan, *Industrial Organization in India* (London: George Allen and Unwin, 1935); Raj K. Nigam, *Managing Agencies in India* (New Delhi: Govt. of India Publication Division, 1957); S.K. Basu, *The Managing Agency System* (Calcutta: The World Press, 1958); Vera Anstey, *Economic Development of India* (London: Longman's Green & Co., 1924); Radhey Shyam Rungta: *Rise of Business Corporations in India, 1850-1900* (Cambridge: Cambridge University Press, 1970); Andrew F. Brimmer, 'Setting of Entrepreneurship in India', *Quarterly Journal of Economics*, Vol. 119, No. 4 (Nov. 1955).
49. Blair B. Kling, 'The Origin of the Managing Agency System in India', *Journal of Asian Studies*, Vol. 26, No. 1 (Nov. 1966). Kling argues, somewhat unconvincingly, that the system originated with Tagore Carr & Co.
50. Rungta, *Rise of Business Corporations* . . . , Chap. 4.
51. Guha, 'More about the Parsi Seths . . . ; Desai, 'The Origins of Parsi Enterprise . . .'; Asiya Siddiqi, 'The Business World of Jamsetjee Jejeebhoy, *Indian Economic and Social History Review*, Vol. 19, Nos. 3 and 4 (July and Dec. 1982), pp. 301-24; K.N. Chaudhuri, 'Markets and Traders in India during the Seventeenth and Eighteenth Century' in *Economy and Society: Essays in Indian Economic and Social History*, ed. by K.N. Chaudhuri and Clive J. Dewey (Delhi: Oxford University Press, 1979), pp. 143-62; Maganlal Vakhatchand, *Amdavadno Itihas* in Gujarati (Ahmedabad: Gujarat Samachar, 1978 rpt.), pp. 135-6.
52. H.A. Antrobus, *The History of the Assam Company, 1853-1953* (Edinburgh: Assam Co., 1957), pp. 12-47; also Perceival Griffiths, *The History of the Indian Tea Industry* (London: Weidenfeld & Nicholson, 1967).
53. L.S.S. O'Malley, *Modern India and the West* (Oxford: Oxford University Press, 1925), pp. 338-9.
54. Moreland, *India* . . . , p. 301.

CHAPTER IV

Japan: Towards Cherry Blossom

HISTORY OFTEN is partial to the winner, cruel to the loser. As the insolent act of gatecrashing into the Bay of Tokyo in 1853 in contemptuous defiance of Shogunal authority by an irrepressible American naval official, Commodore M.C. Perry, thoroughly discredited the Tokugawa regime, its role in the economic transformation of Japan is usually under-recognized. By the same logic, the political system that took control of the country, following the Meiji Restoration—the event signifying the assumption of governmental powers by the emperor in 1868—is given somewhat more credit than it deserves.[1] It should be borne in mind, however, that the task of the Meiji authorities would have been infinitely more arduous had not the political-economic compulsions of the *bakuhan* system already created the necessary pre-conditions for the rise of industrial entrepreneurship. Admittedly, left to themselves the Tokugawas would have done their utmost to keep the society 'frozen' in every respect, thwarting the possibility of an entrepreneurial upsurge, but there is no doubt that but for the objective conditions developed during their long rule, albeit not because but in spite of them, the pace of progress in Japan during the post-Restoration period would have been much slower. It would be fair to suggest with only a slight risk of exaggeration that on the eve of the Meiji Restoration the only thing that stood between the Japanese society and an entrepreneurial breakthrough was the Tokugawa totalitarianism.

It cannot be denied, however, that the conscious and vigorous effort of the Meiji authorities to rally the entire nation behind their plan to achieve equality with the West in the military-economic spheres within the shortest possible time was a significant factor in the ultimate success. But the task of mobilizing the masses would have been far more difficult if Japan had not become a homogeneous and cohesive society centuries before the collapse of the Tokugawa Shogunate, and had not Japanese 'inherited from their feudal period a strong sense of discipline, loyalty, public-mindedness and national unity'.[2] With the enthusiasm accompanying the eclipse of the old, discredited set-up, it was far easier for the new imperial order to carry the entire nation with it. The result was that the slogan 'national prosperity and national strength' symbolizing the will of the new government became a common goal of the entire people. True, the post-Restoration system met with some opposition in certain pockets and there was some confusion initially about the correct strategy to be followed but the opponents were soon humbled and none in the government or outside had any doubt that the only way to meet the challenge of the gate-crashing 'barbarian' West was to catch up with it materially instead of having contempt for it. As Hirshmeirer has rightly pointed out, 'in communicating this newborn faith in modern technology and insustrialization . . . the Meiji officials performed brilliantly'.[3]

This in itself was a big change in the scenario as it raised the status of business endeavours and businessmen in the society. The abolition of all vestiges of feudalism including the four-fold division of the society served the same purpose. No longer was the entrepreneur looked down upon as a social parasite; he came to be seen as the symbol of the national will and an indispensable instrument to achieve the national purpose. Social and occupational mobilities, which were hampered by various ill-conceived restraints imposed under the old dispensation, received a great deal of impetus because the people were now free to pursue a calling of their choice, reside anywhere they chose, and move around in the whole country without let or hindrance. In addition the opening of the country to foreign trade and foreign contact opened up new business opportunities. A new system of education with heavy accent on Western science and technology was introduced and a large number of institutions from the primary schools to the universities and vocational colleges were set up with the declared aim of bringing the fruits of education to every household, nay to every individual. In short, the Meiji administrators consciously and deliberately took a series of steps which within a short period of a decade practically transformed the ideational side of the constellation of forces, augmenting the perception of business opportunities and the motivation to exploit them.

Aware, however, that the social overheads needed for industrial upsurge still had serious gaps, the Meiji government undertook the task of expanding the infrastructural facilities. The national postal service was started in 1871. The first telegraph line was opened in 1869 and, by 1880 all major cities in the country were linked by this facility. The railway era began in 1872 when the eighteen-mile long Tokyo-Yokohama line was inaugurated. There was nothing unusual in these activities, as they were more or less similar to the steps taken by most of the governments in the developed West to facilitate movement and communication, and which were quite consistent with the *laissez faire* doctrine, then a sacred cow in the eyes of most Western policy-makers and economic theorists.

What, however, was unusual in the Meiji approach was the direct participation by government in economic activities which the *laissez faire* apologists frowned upon. A number of enterprises, under public ownership and control, based on equipment and technology were set up. These encompassed diverse areas such as cotton spinning, silk reeling, ship-building, cement, glass, type foundry and coal mining, and were intended to provide an object lesson to the private entrepreneurs, still too timid to risk their resources in unconventional, untried ventures. Besides, loans, either free of interest or at low rates, and subsidies were granted to facilitate establishment of modern ventures under private management and control. In other words, the post-Restoration political order took upon itself the responsibility of introducing and validating modern technology and the modern system of industrial production in the country.[4]

This, however, did not create a hiatus between the government and private enterprise. This was due to three reasons. First, the Japanese people, who had become accustomed to the omnipresence and all-pervasiveness of the state in practically every sphere of national life during the three hundred years of the Tokugawa domination, did not see anything wrong if the government established industrial enterprises, which received less than adequate attention from private business even though they were considered critical for national resurgence. In other words, the change in the political set up did not in any measure divest the government of the legitimacy that the Japanese people had traditionally accorded to it for directing national life in all, including the economic, spheres. Secondly, barring a few areas, such as postal and telegraph services, private enterprise was not excluded from promoting any industry and no field, not even the railways, was reserved for exclusive exploitation by the state, In fact, some of the government undertakings were more in the nature of model factories and pilot plants to demonstrate to the hesitant private capitalists the effectiveness of modern production devices. Generous subsidies and loans to private enterprise to launch ventures in the areas in which the government operated wholly owned units, such as cotton textiles, and the setting up of joint ventures in cooperation with private entrepreneurs in other fields, such as ship-building, served to reinforce the bonafides of the political system as a facilitator instead of a competitor of private enterprise in industrializing the country. And thirdly, as and when the government realized that the purpose with which it had set up industrial enterprises had been served or it could not effectively manage the companies it owned, they were sold to private interests at throw-away prices.

The result was that the kind of confrontation between the government and business that the Western countries witnessed during the early phase of the industrialization process and that many developing countries are experiencing today was almost totally absent from the Japanese scene. In fact, industrial policies and endeavours of the Meiji government gave birth to and nurtured an ideology of partnership, based on mutual trust and interdependence between the state and business—an ideology which is very much in evidence even today. Nowhere else have capitalism and state coexisted so harmoniously and sustained each other so successfully.

As the combined effect of all this, private capital began to show the signs of stirring, and by the end of the first decade of Restoration, private firms began to make their presence felt on the business firmament. Companies arose not only to take over the government undertakings—which, barring a few exceptions such as the Tokyo-Yokohama line, were not doing well—but also to exploit new opportunities in textile, silk filature, shipping, railroads, coal mining, copper-smelting, paper-manufacturing and general trading. Thus, even though the public enterprises failed as profit centres, they did serve as an instrument to validate the effectiveness of modern technology and the modern method of production and distribution.

One of the most impressive developments took place in the area of banking, largely because of government encouragement. Realizing the importance of modern credit institutions for industrial change, the Meiji authorities enacted a legislation in 1872 for the establishment of national banks, patterned after the American system. The initial response of private business to this opportunity was, however, lukewarm because of several disabilities from which the National Bank Act seemed to suffer. When, however, these disabilities were removed by suitable amendments in 1876, banking companies mushroomed with such great speed that by 1879 there were 13 national banks with a total capital of more than 40 million yen.

The progress of private enterprise was admittedly slow in the beginning, but after 1885 both the number of companies and the capital invested increased significantly, with the result that by 1896 the investment of the 50 largest firms amounted to more than 42 million yen. Having burnt its fingers in the initial ventures, the government, of course, refrained from expanding its business activities, but even in the areas in which it continued to operate, the performance of private enterprise was more impressive. In the case of railway construction, for instance, the private companies had laid a total of 1368 miles of lines by 1890, while the government achievement was only one-third of this figure.[5]

Several things are worth remembering in connection with the business growth in post-Restoration Japan. First, the promoters of new enterprises came from diverse social backgrounds. Using the available biographical literature, Hirschmeier has drawn a list of fifty leading enterpreneurs who launched their enterprises between the Restoration and the Sino-Japanese War (1894-5)—a period generally considered to be the most pioneering in Japan's industrial history. The list is based more on qualitative judgement than any definite scientific criteriea, as Hirschmeier himself has conceded, but it can still be accepted as a rough indicator of the trend.[6] Although some of these promoters cannot be identified with any particular social grouping, Hirschmeier's classification does not seem to be too wide off the mark. According to him twenty-three entrepreneurs in his list had samurai background, thirteen came from peasant stocks and twelve were the sons of merchants (with the social origin of the remaining two not being clear). Even if we go by a more conservative estimate, there were at least seventeen samurai. Whatever the case, this estimate runs counter to the common belief that most entrepreneurs of the early Meiji era were drawn from the erstwhile warrior group. Kozo Yamamura's qualitative analysis also disproves this.[7] And yet there is little doubt that the ex-samurai formed a large plurality of those who moved away from their traditional occupations and gravitated to business and industrial pursuits under the impetus provided by the Meiji regime.

This was natural. Belonging to a class whose level of education was higher, the samurai could perhaps better appreciate the significance of emerging opportunities and acquire more easily the requisite expertise and techniques to explore them. With the end of feudalism, their role as the watch-dog of the old political structure had ended and with that had ended their special economic privileges. In their search for an alternative source of livelihood, their appreciation of the industrial opportunities and of their ability to make use of them must have beckoned to a new hope. The traditional sector of the economy would have held little attraction for them because of their deep seated prejudice against trade, and the field at any rate was already monopolized by the merchants. Moreover, promoting new enterprises would have helped the samurai to identify themselves with the nation's goal—which was quite in keeping with their traditional image.

Another factor facilitating the samurai entry into industry was their proximity to the post-Restoration political set up. As they had played a critical role in the Restoration movement, many members of their class were occupying key positions in the government. Because of their proximity with these officials, the samurai entrepreneurs were in a better position to secure and avail themselves of the facilities and concessions that the new government offered for setting up industrial enterprises. This was the origin of the industry-government nexus, which continues to be a distinctive feature of Japanese capitalism to this day. Keeping this in view, George B. Sansom has rightly concluded that it is the samurai 'and not the bourgeoisie, who laid the foundations of a capitalist structure and at the same time developed a political system that bore no resemblance to those which came into force in the advanced industrial countries of western Europe under the influence of a powerful moneyed class'.[8]

This is not to support the popular notion that the samurai businessmen of the early Meiji period were motivated by the lofty spirit of patriotism and national purpose in promoting their enterprises.[9] In most cases, they were primarily driven by mundane consideration of profit and material gain. The same motive seems to have prompted some persons of merchant and peasant categories also to initiate industrial ventures. But their number was understandably smaller because they did not have the advantages the samurai had in terms of education and government connection, and their need for alternative source of livelihood was not as great as that of the samurai. Branching out into relatively new occupations meant an opportunity loss for these classes. With their lower level of education and relatively less exposure to new ideas, they were slow to grasp the meaning of the new environment, and evaluate properly the benefits of new enterprises as compared with their traditional occupations. Perhaps these factors held back the mercantile classes much more than others, for the merchants and their capital remained dominant in the traditional sectors of the economy for quite some time after the Restoration. Hirschmeier, therefore, is right in concluding that 'merchants as a class were the least progressive group of all'.[10]

The less privileged classes remained practically unaffected by the new environment. The artisans, the *Etas* and *Ainus* (the original inhabitants of the country who continued to be subjected to various forms of discrimination in spite of the legal abolition of social inequality by the new government) did not, for instance, figure in the emerging entrepreneuring class. Perhaps their resources, their social position, and their general understanding of the economic forces kept them within their traditional occupational boundaries. This fact notwithstanding, the social composition of Japanese business became much more variegated than ever before within a short period of about two decades after the Restoration. This indicates the measure of occupational mobility the new order had generated.

Secondly, most of the early entrepreneurial initiatives of this period resulted in the rise of firms with diversified interests. As both capital and entrepreneurship were scarce, and the risk involved in setting up enterprises based on modern and hitherto unknown technologies was great, a relatively small group of people, who commanded or could arrange substantial financial resources and possessed requisite managerial capabilities, had a vast expanse of industrial opportunities to exploit in diverse fields. As these persons brought product after product into their entrepreneurial network, their firms gradually developed into multiproduct, multifunction business conglomerates. Most of these new entrepreneurs were closely related to the ruling elite in some way or the other and thus had easy access to government support and help. Although most of the *zaibatsus*, as these conglomerates are known, came into their own after the turn of the century, they had their origin during the early Meiji era. Under the financial and managerial control of business families, the *zaibatsus* established a very tight grip over the industrial life of the nation.

So tight was the stranglehold of these *zaibatsus* on the nation's industrial system that even the non-*zaibatsu* enterprises could not function without the former's support. Most of the non-*zaibatsu* companies were engaged in cotton spinning and remained single-product firms. They were promoted as joint stocks by entrepreneurs with modest resources most of whom did not have the advantage of close connection with the bureaucracy. While it was relatively easy for them to adopt modern methods of production, it was not as easy to procure the raw materials or market their products. For these they had to fall back on the age-old system of distribution that had developed in Japan during the Tokugawa period.

The *tonya* or the middleman, we may recall, was the lynchpin of the distribution system in pre-modern times. In due course his place was taken by trading companies (*sogoshosha*) most of which were an integral part of one *zaibatsu* or the other. So effectively did the *sogoshoshas* control the distribution network that without their help, the cotton spinners could not import raw cotton which Japan did not produce in sufficient quantity, or reach the domestic consumers, much less penetrate the external markets which were exceedingly important because of the limited demand at home. The same pattern operated to some extent in some other consumer goods industries such as sugar refining and flour milling. The process generated a remarkable degree of interdependence between the single-enterprise companies and diversified *zaibatsus*. This was very similar to the situation prevailing before Restoration.[11]

The most impressive manifestation of the continuity of past practices was the method of financing the new industries. Personal savings constituted the major source of finance not only for the *zaibatsu* undertakings but also other companies, with government subsidy or bank loans forming only a small part. This was possible because of a high rate of savings, due in part to surplus-generating agriculture. There may be some disagreement on the rate of growth in the agricultural sector in the early Meiji period, but there is no doubt, as S. Hirashima has suggested, that 'both land productivity and labour input per unit of land increased simultaneously'[12] partly because of the technological bequest of the Tokugawa period and partly as a consequence of various reforms introduced and incentives given by the new government to promote agricultural development. The result was that Japanese agriculture, which was already generating surplus when the feudal era ended, continued with the trend. And as a social ethos which placed a high premium on frugality and austerity had already become a way of life with the Japanese people, the surplus went into savings rather than conspicuous consumption.

Earlier, rural savings found their way largely into what may be called 'rural entrepreneurship'; now a portion of them began to be invested in urban industry. It is significant in this context that all but two of the peasant entrepreneurs in Hirschmeier's list of fifty left their villages and settled down in cities.[13] The new industries also attracted a part of merchant capital on which the agricultural surplus and rural savings must have had a multiplier effect. It is no surprise, therefore, that most of the early spinning mills, set up in or around the regions connected with the traditional cotton trade, were promoted by landlords and merchants.

The enterprises promoted by these entrepreneurs were, by and large, joint-stock companies. They resorted to this method of financing because it facilitated the investment of small savings in industrial undertakings, as their own individual savings would not have been sufficient for their purpose or the risk involved in setting up proprietary firms was too great for them. The development of industrial undertakings boosted up rural savings still further because now a part of the surplus rural labour, previously underemployed for want of any other outlet, could be absorbed by these enterprises. Admittedly, the wages remained low, particularly of young women who constituted a large part of the labour force in the spinning firms, and the worker was subjected to various forms of exploitation, but because of the low cost of living, he was still able to add to the family's resources and thus bolster up its ability to prop up emerging industries directly or indirectly.[14]

All through the above discussion, it is implied that the new enterprises were based on imported technology. In fact, during the initial phases even the technicians were imported to run the machines as Japan lacked trained manpower. But since the foreign technician had to be paid much higher wages and his presence was a painful reminder of Japan's inferiority, Japanese entrepreneurs made vigorous efforts to dispense with external dependence in this crucial area. The transition was so swift that within about two decades after the Restoration, Japanese engineers began to replace the imported personnel in several sectors, such as the railways and textiles, in increasingly larger number and by the turn of the century, the number of foreign technicians working in Japanese manufactories became almost negligible. Admittedly, the Japanese success lay in imbibing and applying technological processes perfected in the West rather than developing new production devices. However, the alacrity with which they were introduced soon after they were developed in the West reflects the state of technological understanding of the Japanese entrepreneurs.

It should also be remembered that wherever possible the Japanese entrepreneurs did exhibit a sense of technological autonomy. This is reflected in at least three different areas: (i) choice of manufacturing devices; (ii) innovations in raw material supply; and (iii) attempt to develop indigenous technologies.

The most conspicuous example of the Japanese sense of technological autonomy was the choice of spinning machinery for their early textile mills. At the time of the birth of the textile industry in that country, the most favoured spinning equipment throughout the world was the mule spindle developed in Great Britain. Quite naturally, this is what the Japanese entrepreneurs installed in their spinning mills and continued to rely on it exclusively up to 1886. In the meantime, a different spinning technology, the ring spindle, was being developed in the United States and it began to come in general use in the American mills by the end of the 1870s. Even though the American device did not surpass the mule spindle in every respect, there was no question about its superiority in at least two respects: it was better suited for spining coarse varieties of yarn and it demanded much less labour efficiency to operate. As Japanese mills were still concentrating on the production of coarse goods and the efficiency of the Japanese labour was not yet comparable to that of his counterpart in industrialized countries, these attractive features of the ring frame caught the attention of the Japanese spinners. The result was that they started switching over to ring within a few years after it had been perfected. In a brief span of two years between 1885 and 1887, the proportion of ring in use in Japanese mills jumped from 13 to 57 per cent. By 1890, ring frame accounted for more than 90 per cent of the total spindles in the Japanese factories and mule practically disappeared from Japan before the end of the first decade of this century. In no other country, not even in the United States where ring was first developed and perfected, was the switchover as swift.[15]

As regards the innovation in raw material creation, the most noteworthy experiment was the blending of various varieties of cotton. European manufacturers had first tried it during the American Civil War when the supply of superior quality from the United States had been interrupted.[16] They, however, gave up the practice after the crisis was over because the quality of goods produced under this process did not suit the consumer's taste in Europe. As the Japanese and the Chinese users—and they were the main buyers of Japanese goods initially—preferred coarse cloth because of the climate, there was no such constraint for the Japanese mills. On the contrary, by mixing various varieties of cotton they could better cater to the taste of their patrons. Because of these advantages, blending of cottons became a fairly general practice in the Japanese mills.

The adoption of ring frame and the practice of mixing cotton, among other things, helped the Japanese spinners to cut production costs without compromising on the quality, produce goods conforming to the requirements of their customers, and sell them at prices lower than others. This would be a major factor in Japan's success in wresting control of the East Asian markets from its competitors, including India which had major presence in these markets well up to the middle of the 1890s.

Perhaps a much better barometer of the Japanese attitude to technology lay in the attempts to develop indigenous know-how. It is not very often recognized that the process started almost on the morrow of the birth of the first cotton mill in that country. A new kind of spindle, known as Garabo spindle, was developed by 1876 which won the first prize at the National Industrial Exhibition held at Tokyo the next year. Drawing power from a water-wheel, it was only a slight improvement over the existing hand spinning system. But it captured a large domestic market because of its low price and continued to be in use in the waste spinning industry even after the spinning mills switched over to better substitutes. Kashima Mampei, the founder of the third textile mill in Japan, used the imported machines at the first stage but later installed indigenous equipment built according to his own designs.

Efforts to develop indigenous weaving technology began a little later. Still Japan had its own powerloom perfected before the end of the century which was almost comparable to the imported machine in quality. This was largely due to the perseverance of an inventor, Sakichi Toyoda, who would also develop and perfect an automatic powerloom of international standard by the mid-1920s. In the meantime, experiments to develop various indigenous devices capable of replacing imported machines in the silk-reeling industry, an important export item so necessary for the nation's economy, had already started around the turn of the century. These, however, would not bear fruit until the mid-1920s by which time Japan would have entered the innovation race with other developing countries in the field of producing chemical fibre and high draft system of spinning.[17]

These contributions to technological development can be roughly placed in two categories: (i) devices which resulted from improving the indigenous know-how already in use such as the Garabo spindles and reeling machines; and (ii) those which resulted from modification of the imported technology to suit the country's needs and environment such as powerlooms, chemical fibres, and high-draft spinning. This twin strategy, as is well known, emerged as the national creed for Japan's industrialists as the years rolled by.

These exercises in technological independence on the part of the Japanese entrepreneurs at the very early stages of industrialization, it must be pointed out, could not have been possible but for the fact that a measure of confidence in their own technological competence had already developed among the Japanese people thanks to the work of the technologists during the Tokugawa era. That a national monarchy aided this process by providing the infra-structure and environment conducive to technological experimentation and advancement is undeniable, but the role of the earlier rulers in laying the solid foundation connot be under-rated.

Education seems to have played a critical role in the process of introduction and adaptation of foreign technology or developing the indigenous ones. With widespread literacy prevailing in Japan at the end of the Tokugawa period, the people needed little persuasion to take advantage of the new educational opportunities opened up by the Meiji authorities, and it would have been easy for the employers to appreciate the value of educated manpower for their organizations. For modern industrial ventures, the services of educated personnel were indispensable as the promoters and the shareholders possessed very little insight into the problems of managing these enterprises. Not only did the business firms begin to recruit in increasingly large numbers the graduates of the institutions of higher learning at home, but they also deputed them for training abroad. These young recruits would gradually rise in the firms' hierarchy and in due course exercise managerial power and control. This is not to suggest that the management and ownership got separated from each other, but there is no doubt that but for the help from these young salaried managers, Japan's experiment in technology transfer would have been far more painful—and far less successful.[18]

II

To illustrate these general remarks about various aspects of business in the early Meiji Japan, let us turn to the actual experiences of some of the principal firms which either emerged or branched out into industrial ventures in this period.

The House of Mitsui[19] was the foremost and the oldest among these. Founded as a mercantile and banking firm in the last quarter of the seventeenth century, the house had amassed a huge fortune during the Tokugawa period through a skillful combination of innovative trading and government connection. Even though of samurai origin, the Mitsuis, like all other merchants, were subjected to all sorts of restrictions by the Tokugawas and when the Restoration movement gained momentum, they went whole hog with the anti-Shogunate forces, supporting the movement with money and in other ways.

The claim that the house thus earned on the gratitude of the

Restoration party brought rich dividends after the Tokugawa eclipse. The Mitsuis acted as one of the financial agents for the new government and later when the National Bank Act was passed in 1872, the Mitsui Bank, held closely by the family and the employees of the house, was among the first major banking companies established on modern lines. Taking advantage of the government failure to run its enterprises, the house acquired a silk filature company and a cotton spinning mill as also a coal mine on highly favourable terms. Two other silk mills were added to the empire in view of the anticipated increase in the demand for silk cloth, and the Kanegafuchi Spinning Mill was acquired from a group of Tokyo merchants. This company would later emerge as the pioneer in producing finer varieties of yarn, although the English specialists had warned against its acquisition. The Mitsuis also acquired the Oji Paper Mill in the face of stiff competition and took control of the Shibaura Iron works.

Perhaps the most significant development in this period of the Mitsui history was the organization of the Mitsui Trading Company (Mitsui Bussan) in 1876. Within a few years, offices of this company were functioning in Great Britain, India, China, France and the United States. If the Mitsuis were the most powerful mercantile concern before the Restoration, they became the most dominant and diversified business conglomerate in the country within two decades after the birth of the new order.

The Mitsui success was partly due to the fact that the house was led during the period by a succession of remarkably sagacious leaders. Minomura Rizaemon (1821-77) who was the principal figure in the house during the period of Japan's transition from feudalism to modernity, and his successors, Masuda Takashi (1848-1938) and Nakamigawa Hikojiro (1854-1901), were very gifted men whose business insights had been considerably sharpened by extensive travel or education abroad. The Mitsuis were among the first business houses in Japan to depute a select group of their personnel for foreign training, to employ university graduates in key positions, and to induct talent into management from wherever they could discover it. Significantly enough, all the three decision-makers whose names are mentioned above came from outside the family.

But the quality of leadership alone does not account for the rise of the house to dizzy heights. Throughout this period, the government of Japan favoured the Mitsuis with a string of concessions. This is clear from the fact that in one single year the house was holding about 3.8 million yen and 460,000 dollars of government money on which no interest was chargeable. By supplying roughly about two-thirds of the army provisions during the Satsuma rebellion, the Mitsuis increased their wealth by at least 400,000 yen in one single year and Hachiroemon Mitsui, the senior partner of the Mitsui Trust, held numerous positions in undertakings in which the government had special interests.

The Mitsuis could reap all these benefits because their leaders maintained very close relationship with key figures in the Meiji government. Minomura was on very intimate terms with Inouye Kaoru, a forward looking and influential member of the cabinet for a good part of this period, who 'could well estimate the knowledge and the political advantages the Meiji government could reap by utilizing the Mitsuis' financial power'. And Mitsui's trust in Inouye was so great that Minomura in his will is believed to have advised his successors that, in any hour of need, they should call upon his friend in the government. This may be folklore but it is true that, without Inouye's timely help, the Mitsui Bank would have collapsed in 1890. He not only secured a loan for the Mitsui Bank from the Bank of Japan, but also persuaded the house to place his nominee in charge of reorganizing the affairs of the house in later years.

Unlike Mitsui, the rise of Mitsubishi[20] was a post-Restoration phenomenon. The *zaibatsu* owed its birth to the enterprising spirit of Iwasaki Yataro (1834-85) who was born in a peasant family but later bought the title of *goshi*, a low ranking samurai. His intention in doing so was to gain access, howsoever limited, to the ruling elite. With the same purpose in view he studied Chinese classics and ethics. His plan eventually succeeded and just a few years before the Restoration, he came in close contact with Yoshida Toyo, a man of progressive ideas, who occupied an influential position in the administration of Tosa, the *han* of which Iwasaki was a native. This contact proved to be a stepping stone for the humble samurai who with Yoshida's help became a minor civil servant. Even though his mentor was killed when Iwasaki was still a minor officer, through his public relations skill and manipulative ability he managed to rise, though through ups and downs, to a respectable level in the *han* bureaucracy.

At the time of the Restoration, Iwasaki was the head of the Nagasaki office of the Industry Promotion Agency (*Keiseikan*). Responsible for purchasing arms for his *han* in his official capacity, he exhibited a great deal of business acumen. For him nothing was unethical which achieved his purpose and he had no qualms in resorting to bribery, trickery, cheating, and so on. So powerful had he become by the time the *han* was abolished in 1871 that he was offered the purchase of all its business including a shipping company which owned a fleet of eleven vessels.

This was the beginning of a career which reached new heights with every passing day. Iwasaki's golden opportunity came when he learnt from his sources in the government that the Meiji authorities were planning to accept the depreciated currency of the *han* at its face value. He quickly acquired a large amount of the old money and made a huge profit by converting it into the Meiji legal tender. This was used to launch the Mitsubishi Shokai (Mitsubishi Trading Firm) in 1873 and expand the shipping business. The authorities were very keen to develop Japanese shipping and eliminate, or at least reduce, the dominance of foreign interests in Japanese waters.

Iwasaki in the meantime had established very close liaison with several key figures in the new government including Okuma Shigenobu. The result was that Iwasaki's shipping concern secured huge subsidies and privileges which, aided by the relentless ruthlessness characteristic of him, enabled him not only to eliminate his competitors, both domestic and foreign, but also build a system of iron-clad monopoly which few in the shipping trade could dare penetrate. By 1877, Iwasaki owned about 80 per cent of all ships in Japan and controlled the entire coastal trade. His business power later aroused great opposition and fierce competition, but he remained almost invincible. His competitors eventually decided to join him in forming a new company—the Nippon Yusen Kaisha (NYK)—by merging all principal shipping concerns. The Mitsubishi Shokai, however, remained the largest single shareholder in the new oligopoly.

Iwasaki also acquired the government shipyard at Nagasaki at a moderate price and the Takashima Coal Mine which, like the shipyard, had been accumulating losses after losses. Both these ventures turned the corner after they came under the Mitsubishi umbrella. Iwasaki also invested in tapping mineral resources in the northern Hokaido region. The Sado gold and Ikuno silver mines also came under his control. With all these efforts, Iwasaki had the satisfaction of having created in a short period of twenty years a business empire second only to Mitsui in power and pelf. And yet at the time of his death in 1885, barely a month after the formation of the NYK, he was regretful that he was leaving nearly two-thirds of his plans unrealized. However, his business philosophy—'Do not take up small projects, engage only in large enterprises'—continued to guide the band of associates he left behind. They carried on the task and led the house into several other enterprises including banking and railways before the century closed.

Another prominent *zaibatsu* builder of the Meiji era was Yasuda Zenjiaro[21] (1838-1921) whose career was somewhat similar to that of Iwasaki. Like the Mitsubishi's founder, he also came from a peasant stock but his father had become a low-ranking samurai by purchasing the title of *goshi* in order to be appointed a minor official in his *han*. The job, however, carried low salary, hardly sufficient for the bare existence of the family. After finishing his early education in a temple school, young Yasuda became a peddler, carrying various kind of acticles on his shoulder and selling them in the villages around Toyama, the capital of his *han*, several miles away from his home. He later left his home, served as apprentice for six years with two small businessmen and then decided to become an independent moneychanger. His meagre savings and six years of experience were his only assets. He could have stayed with his masters—in fact could have even married the daughter of the first—had he accepted their offers, but his ambition had the better of him. His confidence in himself was by no means ill-placed, for by 1868 when the Restoration came, he had already become a man of some means, well known for his accurate judgement of coins and respected for his honesty.

The unsettled conditions following the end of the Shogunate provided a new opportunity to Yasuda. To finance the civil war that came in the wake of the Restoration, the new government issued *dajokan-satsu* (privy counselor's notes) but the instrument was available in such a large quantity that its value soon depreciated by as much as 40 per cent. To remedy the situation the government announced that it would accept the notes at their face value. Yasuda had somehow learnt of the government intention to issue such an order several hours before it was actually promulgated. During these few hours, he bought as many *dajokan-satsu* as he could at the market price and then exchanged them at the face value after the government order came into force. As the bad money began to drive good money out of the nation's treasury, the order was quickly withdrawn but not before Yasuda had taken the fullest advantage of the government's folly and made himself richer several times over. The banker used a similar strategy with the samurai bonds issued by the new government. As these bonds began to depreciate in value because of various reasons, Yasuda purchased a large quantity of them. Fluctuations in their value yielded at least 10 per cent returns to him.

Through these means, he emerged as a fairly rich man by 1874 and was reckoned among the most established and reliable money-changers in the country. It is not at all surprising under these conditions that the Ministry of Justice appointed him as its *qoyokin-gata* (handler of official funds) in 1876. This provided him yet another opportunity to enrich himself because he was free to use the Ministry's money, lodged with him without interest, in any manner he liked as long as he retained the trust of the government. All this wealth stood Yasuda in good stead when the National Bank Act was amended in 1876, clearing many hurdles in the formation of private banking firms. He, jointly with two fellow moneylenders, established the Third National Bank. Three years later when the formation of private banks became still easier, the Yasuda Bank saw the light of day with himself as the sole owner.

These two institutions laid a sound foundation of a large and multiplying fortune. Although Yasuda did not always control the temptation to invest in foolhardy ventures, he on the whole remained a shrewd and calculating business leader and a cautions banker. The government money undoubtedly helped him in expanding his empire, as it did Iwasaki and Mitsui, but it was largely his business acumen and personal qualities of thrift and diligence which placed him among the leading entrepreneurs of the early Meiji era.

Like Mitsui, the house of Sumitomo developed into a powerful *zaibatsu* out of a pre-Restoration trading family which was the official supplier of copper to the *bakufu*. The operation brought large profits but the nature of the business remained unchanged for hundred and fifty years. Flooding, however, dried up the major source of his profit, the Besshi Copper Mine, and only the government subsidy kept the operations alive. This, too, stopped on the eve of the Restoration, and the Sumitomo family would have sold off the mines but for the determination of one Hirose Saihei (1829-1924) to salvage and modernize the business. An adopted child of the manager, he had been with the mines in different capacities ever since he was a young boy and had developed a minute understanding of the intricacy of the business and the problems of the company. A voracious reader, he had also acquired a reasonable good knowledge of Western technology which he continued to replenish through his close association with foreign engineers.

All this stood him in good stead when he proceeded with the task of modernizing the mines. Demonstrating remarkable negotiating abilities, he won the government's support to enable the mines to turn around, launched several welfare schemes with a view to boosting the morale of a restive workforce, and thoroughly reorganized the operation with the help of a foreign engineer. The result was that within less than twenty years after the Restoration, the output of Besshi tripled and this once loss making mine became a prime source of profit. Using this as a base, Hirose led the house into other fields such as real state, machine manufacturing, foreign trade, and banking. All this provided a solid base for future development and eventually Sumitomo emerged as the third largest *zaibastu* in the country—next only to Mitusui and Mitsubishi.

The career of Okura Kihachiro (1837-1928) was in some respects similar to that of Yasuda. Coming from a landowning merchant family, he left his native village at a very young age and set up a trading business in rifles in Edo shortly before the Restoration. As he had supplied arms to the Restoration army, though not out of patriotism but for sheer love for profit, he had earned some claim on the gratitude of the post-Restoration political order. A trip abroad in 1872 inspired him to move into industrial fields, but he continued with his arms-trading business until he had accumulated sufficient finance. The Okura Company which he founded in 1873 was a major supplier of arms to the government during practically all military operations in which Japan was involved in the closing decades of the nineteenth century. So profitable was this business that Okura soon opened branches of his company in London and expanded his operations to Korea and many parts of South-East Asia.

He then moved into a variety of industries—electricity

chemicals, charcoal, lumber, pulp, land reclamation, construction, mining, and insurance. With four holding companies—Okura Construction, Okura Mining, Okura Maritime Insurance and Okura Trading—in its fold, the *zaibatsu's* industrial interests were extensive indeed. Though he often professed economic advancement of the nation to be his paramount concern, seldom would he subordinate his business interests to any other consideration, and though outwardly he lamented his ties with the government, none of his contemporaries with the possible exception of Iwasaki could match his knack to manipulate government connections of the benefit of his empire.

Yet another builder of a business empire in Meiji Japan who rose from a low social origin was Furukawa Ichibei. Son of a poor soyabean cheese peddler, he had been the victim of social inequities that many in his position in feudal Japan had to suffer. Either because of it or in response to the new economic climate generated in the wake of the Restoration, he left home at a very young age and tried to improve his economic prospects through salaried employment and eventually became the chief of the silk export branch of the House of Ono. This house, however, became bankrupt in 1874, and Furukawa's future once again appeared bleak.

He, however, did not lose heart. While working with the House of Ono, he had gained some experience in managing mines. With this experience and a loan from Shibusawa Eiichi (1840-1931), perhaps the most outstanding figure in Japanese business then, to back him up, he bought a decaying copper mine, thoroughly reorganized it with the help of educated young men and converted it into the most modern and efficient copper mine in the entire country. Acquiring mines now became almost an obsession with him and before the end of the century, he owned nineteen mines of copper, silver and gold and a number of mining related enterprises. Some of his concerns had been purchased from the government for ridiculously low prices. Using these as the base, he later moved into other areas such as trading, electricity, rubber, and even railroads.

Unlike Okura and Furukawa, Asano Soichiro (1849-1930) was born in a family which enjoyed a high social standing. The son of a rural physician, he was also the beneficiary of classical samurai education. These advantages, however, were not sufficient to keep him in his village as the post-Restoration environment began to unfold manifold opportunities for material gain. He too, like Okura and Furukawa, left home at an early age and tried to set up manufacturing enterprises without much success. In search of livelihood he eventually landed in Tokyo in 1871 practically penniless, and did a number of odd jobs to earn a living, like selling ice-water in the streets, selling firewood, and even collecting night soil to be sold to peasants as fertilizer.

While eking out a miserable existence in this fashion, he learnt from an engineer that coke could be used as fuel in furnaces of cement works. He then bought an entire pile of coke lying unused at the gas works in Yokohama and sold it to a cement company. This fired his interest in cement production, and with a loan from Shibusawa he eventually acquired the cement company he had sold his first consignment of coke to—the Fukugawa Cement Works. The company had been established by the government but had stopped working because of technical problems, Asano reorganized the company (renamed now as Asano Cement Works), replaced the machinery, and sent his engineers to Germany to upgrade their knowledge of cement production. As a result of all this and because of large government orders, the cement works not only turned the corner but also emerged as one of the most profitable enterprises of its kind in the entire country. With the security and finances his cement venture provided, Asano later moved into shipping and ship-building, mining, iron works, power generation and a host of other lines.[22]

There were many other *zaibutsu* of varying sizes. However, the cases we have selected seem to represent different typologies of *zaibatsu*-builders in the early Meiji era. Others of their ilk may be identified in some degree with one of these types. The accounts of the *zaibatsus* discussed here may provide a sufficiently good idea of the emerging structures of big business in Japan and the strategic approaches of the business leaders during the Meiji era.

Certain features are common to all these typologies. Practically all of them benefited from their association with the government. All of them entered a variety of industrial fields, and most of them had their own banks, symbolizing a strategic combination of industrial and finance capitalism. By and large, they were less interested in light industries and concentrated on key sectors such as engineering, transportation, mining, chemicals, metallurgicals and electricity. Even though their leaders came from different social backgrounds and had different levels of education, all of them had some understanding of business development in the West, and all of them broke away from the dead weight of tradition. They were all ruthless competitors and restless seekers of economic power, just like the 'robber barons' in post-Civil War America, but unlike the American businessmen they all cooperated with the government and benefited a great deal from this cooperation.

All the *zaibatsu* builders had one more thing in common, despite the differences in their entrepreneurial visions and personalities. Without exception, all of them retained iron-fist control over their enterprises and abhorred the joint-stock form. But the joint stock principle did gain a measure of acceptance thanks to the rise of small investors who individually were not in a position to launch modern ventures. Shibusawa Eiichi[23] (1840-1931) perhaps did more than any single individual to popularize this form of corporate ownership. Son of a rich farmer, who also dealt in trade and moneylending, he had received a literary education and inherited considerable business insight. Both because of his education and travel abroad, he had become a great admirer of Western education, Western ideas and Western forms of enterprise. For some time after the Restoration, he served in the Ministry of Finance, but later resigned his position and accepted the presidentship of the First National Bank. From this vantage position, he exerted a powerful influence on the course of industrial development of the country at the formative stage. Not only did he help a number of entrepreneurs to set up modern industries, but he also played a critical role in the birth of several joint-stock companies. In collaboration with the House of Mitsui, he organized a shipping concern to break the monopoly of Iwasaki. The company achieved its purpose only partially and was eventually merged with the NYK which continued to remain under the domination of the ruthless *zaibatsu*-builder.

The success of Shibusawa's other enterprises, however, served to establish the viability of the joint-stock principle and create the kind of demonstration effect needed to overcome the vacillation of a large number of small investors in using the emerging business opportunities. He was the chief promoter of the Osaka Spinning Mill (1883), the first large cotton textile firm, which did so well in the very first year of operations that as many as 33 new mills were started in the next eight years. Likewise the Oji Paper Mill, founded by Shibusawa in 1875, was the largest and most prestigious company in its field. He was also instrumental in the establishment of a brick factory, several national banks, a fertilizer company and a glass works. All his enterprises were not equally successful—in fact some could never overcome their difficulties—but if a horde of new entrepreneurs came to the fore to form joint-stock companies, a large part of the credit must go to the leadership and entrepreneurial zeal of persons like Shibusawa.

Whatever the form of ownership, the Japanese industrial concerns in their approaches to organizational structure continued to exhibit many essential features of the medieval commercial firms, and the managerial behaviour and ethos continued to be informed by the same basic principles. Controlled by business families, the *zaibatsus* were very much like the *ie* of the olden times in which the chief was seen as the fountainhead of all critical decisions. The joint stock companies were not very different in this respect. And all companies looked upon their employees as a lifetime resource; respect for seniority was an important principle governing career advancement in all of them; and group orientation rather than individual drive informing the conduct of managerial workforce remained the general pattern. Thus, even though the character of the Japanese business and economy underwent a virtual transformation after the Restoration, the Japanese business system remained almost intact in its organizational aspects. This was so because the penetration of the modern method of production into the economy made little dent on the basic tenets of social interaction, and these continued to be reflected in business life as much as in any other sphere.

All this—the exertions of the government, *zaibatsu*-builders and promoters of joint-stock companies—was a reflection of that 'new deal in emotion' which, according to Gerschenkron, is the first prerequisite for 'the great and sudden industrialization effort' in a backward country[24] as Japan was at the end of the *ancien regime*. Within less than a generation, however, the Japanese economy had reached the 'take off' stage if we accept Rostow's judgement.[25] By the middle of the 1890s, the nation's industrial horizon had become not only extensive but also fairly varied, comprising light industries such as cotton textile and silk reeling, hemp and flax, transportation and capital goods industries such as railways, shipping, shipbuilding, and mining, and chemical industries like glass, cement, match, sulfur, paper, and fertilizer, as well as various kind of credit institutions. Some progress had been made in even more sophisticated lines such as iron and steel and machine making. Though the real development of these basic industries would have to wait for another decade or so, the stage for their growth had already been set in the sense that the industries needing these inputs had already attained a measure of maturity.

It the progress of industrial entrepreneurship was so rapid during the period, it was largely because Meiji Japan had inherited from the earlier period a near-mobilized situation for entrepreneurial upsurge. The policies and the programmes of the Meiji government undeniably helped but it is the solid, though hidden at the moment, strength with which Japan set off on its industrial journey that explains, more than anything else, its rapid pace. Seen in a proper perspective, thus, what was achieved during the early Meiji period was the culmination of developments spanning over three centuries rather than the fruits of efforts covering only three decades.

NOTES

1. For a recent study in this category of works see, Yukihiko Kiyokawa, 'Entrepreneurship and Innovations in Japan: An Application of the Experience of Technological Development in the Textile Industry', *Developing Economies*, Vol. 27, No. 3 (Sept. 1984) pp. 211-36.
2. J. Hirschmeier, *Origins of Entrepreneurship in Meiji Japan* (Cambridge: Harvard University Press, 1974), p. 289.
3. Ibid., p. 112.
4. The efforts made by the post-Restoration government to create a better climate for enterprise are discussed in a large number of works. Kamekichi Takahashi, *The Rise and Development of Japan's Modern Economy* (Tokyo: The Jiji Press, 1969) is among the most comprehensive treatments. K. Kobayashi and M. Kobayashi, 'Government Promotion of Manufacturing as a Precondition for Industrialization' in *Government and Business*, ed. by K. Nakagawa (Tokyo: University of Tokyo Press, 1980), pp. 25-53 and Takeaki Teratani, 'Japanese Business and Government in the Take off Stage' in the same volume, pp. 57-8 are excellent summaries.

5. Keiichiro Nakagawa, 'Business Strategy and Industrial Structure in Pre-World War II Japan' in *Strategy and Structure of Big Business*, ed. by K. Nakagawa (Tokyo: University of Tokyo Press, 1978), pp. 3-38 has discussed these points in greater detail. See also Yoshi Tsurumi, *Japanese Business* (New York: Praeger Publishers, 1978), pp. 13-50.
6. Hirschmeier, *Origins of Entrepreneurship* . . . , pp. 248-9.
7. Kozo Yamamura, *A Study of Samurai Income and Entrepreneurship* (Cambridge: Harvard University Press, 1974), pp. 137-87.
8. George B. Sansom, *The Western World and Japan* (New York: Alfred Knopf, 1951), pp. 110-11.
9. Major studies supporting this viewpoint are, G. Ranis, 'The Community Centered Entrepreneur in Japanese Development', *Exploration in Entrepreneurial History*, Vol. 8, No. 2 (1955); Hirschmeier, *Origins of Entrepreneurship* . . . , and B.K. Marshall, *Capitalism and Nationalism in Pre-war Japan: The Ideology of the Business Elite* (Stanford: Stanford University Press, 1967).
10. Hirschmeier, *The Origins of Entrepreneurship* . . . , p. 255.
11. K. Nakagawa, 'Business Strategy and Industrial Structure . . .', pp. 7, 14. For trading companies see Yushihara Kunio, *Sogo Shosha The Vanguard of the Japanese Economy* (Tokyo: Oxford University Press, 1982).
12. S. Hirashima, 'Growth, Equity and Labour Absorption in Japanese Agriculture' in *Labour Absorption and Growth in Agriculture: China and Japan*, ed. by Shigeru Ishikawa *et al.* (Bangkok: International Labour Organization, 1982), pp. 65-6.
13. Hirschmeier, *The Origins of Entrepreneurship* . . . , p. 255.
14. Thomas C. Smith, 'Landlords and Rural Capitalists in the Modernization of Japan', *Journal of Political Economy*, Vol. 14, No. 2 (1956); see also K. Nakagawa, 'Business Strategy and Industrial Structure . . .', pp. 14-18.
15. Kiyokawa, 'Entrepreneurship and Innovations in Japan . . .', for technological modification in another industry see, Yukihiko Kiyokawa, 'Transplantation of the European Factory System and Adaptations in Japan: The Experience of the Tomioka Model Filature' (Discussion Paper No. 98, Institute of Economic Research, Hitotsubashi University, 1984).
16. Dwijendra Tripathi, 'The United States and India: Economic Links, 1860-1900', Ph.D. Dissertation (University of Wisconsin, 1963), p. 70.
17. Kiyokawa, 'Entrepreneurship and Innovations . . .'.
18. Shinichi Yonekawa, 'University Graduates in Japanese Enterprises before the Second World War', *Business History*, Vol. 24, No. 2 (July 1984), pp. 193-218; see also Hirschmeier and Yui, *Development of*

Japanese Business, 1600-1983 (London: George Allen and Unwin, 1985), pp. 162-70.

19. Olando D. Russell, *The House of Mitsui* (Westport: Greenwood Press, 1939). The quotation about Inouye's connection with Minomura is on p. 164; John G. Roberts, *Mitsui* (New York: Waterhill, 1973).
20. Unlike Mitsui, a comprehensive history of Mitsubishi is not available in English. The account given here is based on Yamamura, *Study of Samurai Income and Entrepreneurship* (Cambridge: Harvard University Press, 1974), pp. 143-53, which has drawn on a large number of authentic sources.
21. Ibid., pp. 153-9.
22. The accounts of Sumitomo, Okura, Furukawa and Asano are based on Hirschmeier, *Origin of Entrepreneurship* . . . , pp. 226-40 and Hirschmeier and Yui, *The Development of Japanese Business* . . . .
23. Hirschmeier, *Origins of Entrepreneurship* . . ., pp. 167-75, 187-95.
24. Alexander Gerschenkron, 'Economic Backwardness in Historical Perspective' in *The Progress of Underdeveloped Area,* ed. by Bert F. Hoselitz (Chicago: University of Chicago Press, 1952), p. 24.
25. According to W.W. Rostow, Japan's take off occurred during 1878-1900, *Stages of Economic Growth* (Cambridge: Cambridge University Press, 1960). Other scholars have differed only slightly. S. Kuznets, for instance, determines this period to be 1874-79, *Modern Economic Growth: Rate, Structure and Spread* (New Haven: Yale University Press, 1966); and K. Okhawa and Rosovsky place it between 1886 and 1905, 'A Century of Japanese Economic Growth' in *The State and Economic Enterprise in Japan,* ed. by W.W. Lockwood (Princeton: Princeton University Press, 1965).

CHAPTER V

India: The Slow Germination

THE NEW CLIMATE for enterprise that had brought a new breed of Bengali entrepreneurs to the fore in the second quarter of the nineteenth century spread to other part of India in the wake of the expansion of the burgeoning British authority. To ensure an affective governance of the conquered land it was imperative for the new rulers to adopt various administrative measures, some of which have been outlined at the end of the third chapter. These incidentally served to enlarge the size of the market and provide greater security for investment. At the same time, European liberalism continued to make slow inroads into Indian life and thought, thanks to the expanding opportunities for modern education and growing interaction between the Indians and Englishmen at various levels, striking gentle, but effective blows to the hard cakes of Indian customs and dogmas. In other words, the material as well as the ideational aspects of the constellation of forces impinging on business behaviour were slowly and gradually undergoing a metamorphosis in the entire country, though in varying degrees, around the mid-nineteenth century, broadening in the process the vista of business opportunities.

However, the Bengalis who had burnt their fingers in the Indo-British partnerships of the 1830s and 40s remained too cautious to take further initiatives, or found opportunities in civil services much more alluring.[1] And in those parts of the country such as the north and south where business had made but limited progress for various reasons, the message of the slowly transforming environment was still too feeble to make a breakthrough. It was in western India—the Bombay-Gujarat region where some measure of capital accumulation had already taken place as a result of a long history of trade and commerce—that the new Indian entrepreneurial spirit began to manifest itself noticeably.

Even in these regions, however, the Indians kept aloof from the fields in which the British entrepreneurs has already gained a foothold, such as plantation and coal mining. Because of climatic reasons or proximity to the sources of raw material, these industries could develop only in eastern India and the sheer distance might have discouraged western Indian entrepreneurs from developing a meaningful interest in them. It is also possible that because of their lack of experience with industrial enterprise, they did not feel sufficiently confident to compete with British entrepreneurs in these fields. The same reasons seem to have discouraged the Indians from entering the jute industry which started developing around the mid-1850s. For one thing, Bengal where the jute plant was cultivated in abundance, thanks to favourable climate, was too far away for the capitalist in the Bombay-Gujarat region, given the prevailing facilities for transport. Besides, the Indians could not have hoped to match the technical capabilities of the Scottish entrepreneurs who had experimented successfully to produce manufactured goods out of Indian jute fibre ever since 1832 and thus had accumulated a store of experience in this field.[2] When the Crimean War (1854-6) cut off supplies of Russian hemp from Dundee, the principal centre of flex and hemp cloth manufacture, they were forced to turn their attention to the possibility of setting up jute mills in India and succeeded so admirably that Indian jute manufacturing became their almost exclusive preserve. Two major fields, cotton textile and steel, held little interest for British entrepreneurs, perhaps because Britain already had become a world leader in these. It is in these fields that the emerging native entrepreneurship expressed itself most vigorously.

Initiative to develop both these industries were taken by the Parsees. A member of this community, Cowasji Nanabhoy Davar, established the first cotton mill in 1854 in the fast developing city of Bombay. Belonging to a family of merchants, he had extensive trading connection with East Asia, was a broker to two English commercial firms, and had been active in promoting a few modern banks in Bombay. He was also instrumental in forming a steam navigation company, organising a firm to import machinery and opening the first steam powered cotton press in Bombay.[3] Davar and his fellow Parsees held the controlling shares in his—and India's—maiden industrial venture, but businessmen belonging to other communities also contributed to its share capital. Machinery and technicians came from Lancashire and the shareholders, through a deed of agreement, entrusted the management to Davar on certain terms and conditions which anticipated the provisions that would later become the essential features of the managing agency system in its fully developed form. Although the city's business circles were skeptical about the future prospects of the venture, the Bombay Cotton Spinning and Weaving Mills became an instant success and a source of inspiration to many other merchants, most of them belonging to Davar's own community, to follow his lead. The result was that by 1860, within a short span of six years. Bombay city could boast of at least ten textile units.

The industry probably would have developed still faster but for the intervention of the American Civil War which kept the Bombay business environment completely out of gear between 1860 and 1865—creating an unprecedented high demand for Indian cotton in Britain, which resulted in the worst ever speculation the city has witnessed in its entire history, followed by the sudden collapse of the entire economic structure erected on the ephemeral prosperity of the boom years. As the city recovered from the trauma, the industry resumed its progress and was firmly established by 1875 despite many adverse factors—opposition from the powerful Manchester lobby and unhelpful governmental policies being the most formidable. Not only a large internal market but also growing demand for Indian goods in China and Japan made this development possible.[4] Although persons belonging to other castes and communities contributed to the growth of the Bombay textile industry, the pioneering role undoubtedly was played by the Parsees.

A Parsee was also the father of the Indian iron and steel industry. Jamshetji Nusserwanji Tata was attracted to the field was early as the last quarter of the nineteenth century in spite of the failure of many dreamers preceding him. Like Davar, he too came from a family which had long been active in trade but his business dealings with English firms and his exposure to the outside world were much more extensive and his educational attainments much more impressive. Making his industrial debut with a cotton textile company, Tata was soon attracted to the idea of manufacturing steel which must have seemed impossible to all his contemporaries. How he was hampered by irksome and complicated prospecting regulations, how he used his personal links with British authorities to get the legislations modified, how he recruited his technicians and imported machinery from the United States, and how his efforts finally fructified in the form of the Tata Iron and Steel Company at what is now Jamshedpur in the first decade of the present century need not be repeated. What is important is that a less imaginative and less daring entrepreneur would have thrown in the towel in the face of the formidable hurdles that any attempt to set up a steel mill in India had to contend with then. But Tata's vision, perseverance, and resolve to realise his dream and his unshaken faith in himself and his mission survived many a frustration and many a failure.[5]

The cultural determinists may be tempted to attribute these pioneering initiatives of the Parsees to their religion and culture. For, surely enough, there is no injunction against pursuing the business profession under Zoroastrianism, the religion of the Indian Parsees—not even for those who, like the Tata's ancestors, performed priestly functions. And a large number of Parsees had indulged in commercial pursuits from the beginning of their history in India, investing the profession with unquestioned social legitimacy. Some others may seek to explain the Parsee lead in launching industrial enterprises to their deviant status in Indian society.[6] For, the community indeed has been very conscious of its distinct social identity in Indian society,[7] and has always jealously guarded its distinctiveness against the forces of possible erosion.

The cultural explanation of the early entry into modern industries by the Parsees, however, would be misleading. The simple fact that the founder of the first textile mill of Ahmedabad—which would soon develop into the nation's second largest cotton manufacturing centre deserving the epithet the 'Manchester of India' because of the concentration of the mill industry—belonged to the mainstream of the Indian society, whose caste background should have kept him away from the dirty field of business, is a sufficient proof of it. Ranchhodlal Chhotalal was a Nāgar Brahman, a caste group concentrated mostly in urban centres (hence 'nāgar' as derivative of 'nagar' meaning city) The Nagars were the first in Gujarat to take good advantage of new educational opportunities and imbibe progressive, liberal influences. Ranchhodlal himself can be regarded as highly educated man for his times with good command over Sanskrit, English and Persian languages. Like most Nagar boys, he was trained to be a civil servant and, like most educated Nagars, he started his professional career in the civil service, rising to the highest position open to an Indian in the mid-nineteenth century. This gave him an opportunity to develop friendly contacts with English officers including some who had close links with textile manufacturers and machinery-makers back home. With his imagination fired by information gleaned from these officers, Ranchhodlal dreamt of starting a cotton company in Ahmedabad and carried on extensive correspondence with several knowledgeable persons a few years before Davar floated his mill in Bombay. Hampered by the lack of capital, however, he had to wait for more than a decade before he finally succeeded in floating his mill company in 1858 which started production three years later.[8]

Exposure to new ideas and values was the common factor between the Bombay-based pioneers of industrial enterprises and the father of the textile industry at Ahmedabad, even though they followed different religions and were subject to different cultural traditions. The Parsees from the very beginning of the British operations in India had developed very close ties with alien merchants who utilized their services as middlemen. The Bombay Parsees like the Nagars in Gujarat were the first to appreciate the value of learning English and their contacts with British interests in India exposed them to European cultural influences, They even adopted some aspects of Western ways of life. Business had been their traditional occupation, but it was their contact with new ideas and new business techniques that led then to realize the meaning of the changing environment and emerging opportunities in industrial fields.[9] The same was true about the Ahmedabad entrepreneur although business was a new experience for him. It is worth pointing out that even though Ranchhodlal remained the undisputed leader of the business life of Ahmedabad throughout his life, his adherence to the religious rituals and practices was as steadfast as that of any orthodox Nagar of his times.[10] Neither he nor his contemporaries saw any contradiction between his caste background and his new occupation.

Significantly enough, those who immediately followed the Bombay and the Ahmedabad pioneers in the industrial arena had been influenced by the same forces, though to a much lesser extent, that had inspired the birth of the initial ventures. In Bombay, practically all mills up to the beginning of the 1870s were set up by the Parsees. The first non-Parsee to take up cotton manufacturing in that city was Khatau Makanji whose Khatau

Makanji Spinning and Weaving Limited came into existence in 1874—full twenty years after the establishment of the first mill. He was a Bhatia merchant whose family had migrated from the Kutch region of Gujarat. Although the community to which he belonged was very backward educationally and culturally, he himself was counted among a small group of progressive Bhatias and had close business links with Parsee merchants.[11] In Ahmedabad, the immediate emulator of Ranchhodlal's example was Bechardas Laskari who belonged to the landholding community of Kanbis. His family, as suppliers of commissariat to the military, had come in contact with British officers in India, and thus developed some appreciation of the value of modern industries.[12]

The entrepreneurial vision of these early pioneers seem to have had some relationship with the level of their exposure to or appreciation of new ethos and values. Davar, for instance, remained content with his success in promoting a solitary industrial firm and made no attempt to either expand his textile empire or diversify into new fields. Also, there was nothing very innovative in his managerial style and practices. Nor were other promoters, Parsee or non-Parsee, of textile companies in Bombay very different from Davar in these respects. In contrast, Tata, with his much deeper understanding of industrial enterprises in the West, thanks to his wide travels and direct interaction, demonstrated much greater propensity for business risk and managerial innovation. His ambitious steel venture was indeed of a class apart, but even his textile firms bore the imprint of a man who was far ahead of his contemporaries.

Not only did he continue to expand his textile empire by acquiring sick units and turning them around, he also had the distinction of being the first millowner in the country to introduce new technological devices in his companies, experiment with unconventional managerial structure, and extend to the workforce the benefit of many welfare measures unheard of in the Indian industrial circles till then.[13] Ranchhodlal's exposure to the outside world was much less direct than Tata's, but whatever understanding of modern industries he had gained through his contacts with English officials and engineers in India was sufficient to lead him to promote another mill, introduce in the Ahmedabad mill industry the production of superior quality yarn, and even attempt to launch a company for mining coal and iron ore.[14] His follower Laskari's dreams and achievements in comparison remained much more modest.

The success of the pioneering textile ventures had little immediate impact on the business decision of those traders and moneylenders in Bombay and Ahmedabad who were late in waking up to the value of new educational opportunities or slow in coming in contact with new ideas and mores. These elements continued to remain immersed in their traditional pursuits. Most of the Hindu and Jain merchants, who still dominated the Indian business horizon, belonged to this category. The Bhatia and Kutchhi traders in Bombay took about two decades to realize the profit potential of industrial ventures and entered the field only after the industry had been firmly established. Some of them—like Veerjeevan Madhowdas, a rich Bania merchant and banker—did invest in the ventures promoted by others, but the people belong-ing to traditional Hindu business castes were really drawn to the textile industry only after 1875.[15]

Likewise, mercantile interests in Ahmedabad and Baroda refused to do anything with the cotton industry when the Nagar pioneer approached them with the proposal to support his industrial scheme, leading Ranchhodlal to lament in despair that those who had ideas had no money and those who had money were devoid of imagination. Had the Jain and Vaishnava Banias of the city joined hands with Ranchhodlal, Ahmedabad, and not Bombay, perhaps would have had the distinction of having India's first cotton mill. In fact, in spite of their financial power, these elements waited on the sidelines for almost twenty years after the birth of the first cotton company in their city and entered the field only after Ranchhodlal's and Bechardas's experiments had demonstrated the unquestionable profit potential of the new line.[16]

This was a perfectly rational reaction on the part of the commerical interests. The interest rates both in Bombay and Ahmedabad were quite high, ranging between 12 and 22 per cent, and moneylending and trading promised safe and high returns. Investing in industrial ventures with still uncertain future would have meant a possible opportunity loss for them, involving a trade-off between a sure and familiar source of quick profit and an uncertain and untried field the intricacies of which they hardly knew. However, once the reservations about the future of industrial enterprises yielded place to faith in their profit potential, thanks largely to the demonstration effect of the pioneering ventures, the moneylenders and traders in both centres of textile production entered the field with a bang and made their presence felt on the industrial front. While in the Bombay industry, the Hindu merchants soon came to occupy a place second only to that of the Parsees, in Ahmedabad the Jain and Vaishnava Banias emerged as the dominant group.[17]

Impressive as this progress was, the fact remains that Indian industrial entrepreneurship during the first fifty years after the birth of the first cotton mill had manifested itself convincingly only in one area—cotton textiles—and it was still concentrated by and large in a single geographical region—western India—when the century ended. Tata's Empress Mills at Nagpur was among the few Indian promoted companies located out of this region.[18] The success of the western Indian entrepreneurs, however, did inspire some people in other parts of the country to promote cotton manufacturing. The initiative of a group of Punjabi Hindus, belonging to diverse social and occupational background, to organise a cotton manufacturing company in their area in 1888 was perhaps the earliest of such attempts. Because of several difficulties, their scheme took a long time to fructify but it eventually bore fruit in the form of the Delhi Cloth and General Mills Company Ltd. which started production in 1891. Significantly enough, few of its promoters had much prior experience of business—not even the ancestors of Lala Shri Ram under whose leadership the company would achieve great heights later. Though Agrawal Bania by caste, most members of this family had been in police service. Most other promoters too were closely connected with the bureaucracy and thus had absorbed 'some elements of Western culture, some ways of Western thinking'.[19]

In the meantime, persons exposed to new influences or equipped with requisite technical skills began to respond creatively to emerging industrial opportunities in more challenging fields. Surprisingly, even the Bengalis, who had meekly conceded to the Scottish entrepreneurs the right to develop jute manufacturing in their own backyard, were slowly emerging from the slumbering stupor they had fallen into after the business failures of the 1840s. This is evidenced by the career of Rajendra Nath Mookerjee. Born in a Brahmin family and trained as an engineer, he first joined a

Bengali contracting firm, specializing in light engineering jobs, as a partner and helped his company complete in record time a large pipe-laying contract for the Calcutta Corporation. He later met one Acquin Martin, the Calcutta agent of a London firm dealing in general stores and metals, who like Mookerjee was basically interested in engineering schemes. Martin, therefore, parted company from his London principals, and joined hands with Mookerjee and two other Englishmen to form Martin & Co. in 1872. It soon grew into a reputable engineering firm which would in due course acquire the prestigious Burn & Co. of Calcutta, and take possession of the iron works of the Bengal government. So valuable was Mookerjee's contribution to developing Martin Burn & Co. that after Martin's death he became the senior partner and undisputed leader of the firm.[20]

Another Bengali whose industrial initiative seems to have been inspired by his professional training was Praful Chandra Ray. Having obtained a Ph.D. degree in Chemistry from the University of Edinburgh in 1888, he began his career as an assistant professor at Calcutta's prestigious Presidency College. Not content with mere teaching, however, he decided to manufacture such drugs and pharmaceuticals as required small capital and had a good market. With the help of some friends and associates he started his operations in 1892 and later purchased a small laboratory which developed within less than a decade into the Bengal Chemicals Limited, regarded as 'one of the most go-ahead young enterprises' in the province. Ray's was one of the most successful attempts to develop the chemical industry in the last quarter of the nineteenth century and his firm was the only firm under complete Indian control and management.[21]

Unknown to Ray, another Chemistry professor at the other end of the country was trying to use his professorial knowledge to further the industrial cause. He was Tribhuvandas Kalyandas Gajjar, a carpenter by caste, who after obtaining an M.Sc. degree in Chemistry from the Elphinstone College, Bombay, had joined the Baroda College as a professor in 1886. Being 'more interested in applying science for industrial purposes' he conducted many experiments in makeshift laboratories and later set up two small chemical factories at Bombay, one of these being in collaboration with one of his students, A.S. Kotibhaskar. These factories produced chemicals used in polishing precious stones, spirit, pharmaceuticals, toilet articles and a few drugs. These ventures were not as successful as Ray's Bengal Chemicals but they did pave the ground for the rise of the Alembic Chemical Works at Baroda. Impressed by Gajjar's and Kotibhaskar's efforts, a rich and educated landholder, B.D. Amin, decided to promote this pioneering firm with the help of the two scientists who sold off their factories to the new company. Formally registered in 1907, Alembic was one of the four chemical firms in the whole of the country, and only one in western India, then.[22]

In another part of western India around the same time, a Maharashtrian Brahmin, Laxmanrao K. Kirloskar was struggling to create an enterprise based on his technical expertise. Belonging to a family of petty civil servants, he was trained as a technical draughtsman and started his career as a teacher of mechanical drawing at the Victoria Jubilee Technical Institute, Bombay. He used this opportunity to develop his technical skills; all his spare time was often spent in the Institute's workshop to understand the structure and operation of various machines. He also honed his engineering expertise through voracious reading of books and journals. By 1890, he had earned a certain measure of reputation for his knowledge of mechanical intricacies. None of this, however, helped his career prospects; he was denied promotion simply because senior posts in the Institute were not open to Indians. Resentful of this blatantly racial policy, he quit the job and decided to earn a living through his own independent efforts, using his mechanical talents. Through a series of trials and errors, spanning over almost a decade, Laxmanrao eventually hit upon the idea of producing improved agricultural implements at the turn of the century. Given the innate conservatism of the Indian farmer and the Brahmin entrepreneur's meagre resources, even this did not prove to be an easy enterprise. But Laxmanrao persevered and his firm, Kirloskar Brothers, had achieved some degree of stability before the First World War.[23]

All these, admittedly, were examples of sporadic entrepreneurial ventures, launched by professionally trained persons, which required much greater insights into manufacturing processes than cotton textiles. They, nevertheless, were indicative of how Indians with requisite capabilities and knowledge of industrial transition in the West could perceive new opportunities even in unconventional lines. And these like textile companies represented a purely autonomous development. For, nothing in the attitude of the then government towards industrialization could have encouraged or excited the Indian entrepreneurs. Most Western economists of this period advocated the *laissez faire* doctrine which eminently suited the colonial-imperial character of the Indian regime. Even though the British authorities had no compunction in deviating from its essential tenets wherever the imperial interests so demanded,[24] the doctrine provided philosophical justification for the government to remain scrupulously aloof and refrain from giving any direct impetus to industrial development. Improving infrastructural facilities and maintaining law and order were considered to be the only legitimate functions of the government, and these were quite consistent both with the *laissez faire* doctrines and imperial needs. The colonial government also had to contend with pressure from the manufacturers at home to ensure that the rise of modern industries in the colonies did not pose, even remotely, a challenge to Britain's industrial supremacy. Throughout the latter half of the nineteenth century, therefore, the import duties on textile goods and excise levies on India's domestic production were so adjusted as to deny the colony any competitive advantage resulting from the easy availability of cheap labour and raw material.[25] Yet, undaunted by the government's indifference to India's industrial development and despite explicit discrimination on occasions against its industrial interests, the new breed of entrepreneurs, capable of perceiving and exploiting new opportunities, continued to multiply.

Most of the nineteenth century Indian entrepreneurs, however, belonged to western India, and most of their enterprises were still confined to this region which was the first to experience the stirrings of factory production. Commercial interests in other regions away from the major theatres of industrial change, who did not have the benefit of exposure to new ideas and education or to the demonstration effect of the industrial accomplishments of their peers, continued to pursue their traditional business activities. In Calcutta the Marwaris, who had a stronghold on the money markets, remained content with trading and usury, and so was the case with the Chettiars in south India.[26] Entrenched firmly in their traditional occupations and profiting by high interest rates, these sections needed greater and more concrete inducements to realize that a shift to industry would not mean an opportunity loss for them but just the reverse.

II

Such inducements came in the first quarter of the twentieth century. First, the Swadeshi movement gave a new fillip to the demand for Indian goods in the country. Arising out of a political reaction against Lord Curzon's ill-conceived decision to divide Bengal province in 1904, the Swadeshi agitation advocated the use of goods produced domestically in place of the imports. Whether the Indian business interests grasped the political message of the movement is doubtful, but they fully understood the economic meaning of it. Most producers of textiles expanded their production capacity to meet the augmented demand; there were many new entrants in the field; and Tata's steel venture, launched finally in 1907, drew enthusiastic support from Indian investors.[27] In no other field did the Swadeshi movement make much of an impact because no other industry had made much progress in India. By the time the Swadeshi wave began to recede, the First World War, disrupting imports and creating huge internal demand for indigenous products, opened up new vistas of profit for Indian industrialists.

More important than all this, the period witnessed the emergence of a strong business pressure group, conscious of its distinctive identity, confident of its power, and determined not to play second fiddle to the British business interests operating in India any more. It gradually drew closer to the nationalist movement, which in the meantime was becoming more and more militant, without alienating the government of the day. With the support of the nationalist political forces, it fought against some of the discriminatory measures affecting the Indian industries adversely—such as the excise duties imposed on the domestic production of textile goods in 1892 to counterbalance the import duties on British products—and forced the government to abolish them.[28] Recognizing the new political reality, the government also modified its adherence to the *laissez faire* doctrine and introduced the policy of discriminating protection under which selected Indian industries, satisfying certain criteria, would be provided some measure of security against foreign competition by means of protective tariffs. As the *laissez faire* ideology had lost much of its lustre at home by this time, the colonial regime had little difficulty in introducing this salutary change in its industrial policy. Also, the currency situation, which had remained fluid and uncertain almost up to the end of the first quarter of the twentieth century became more stable at long last.[29]

Cumulatively, these developments reduced the risk in launching modern industrial ventures. The mercantile interests as a result cast off their hesitation and, having at their disposal enormous capital accumulated through trading operations, entered the industrial arena. The rise of most of the industrial houses prominent in Indian business today can be traced back to the period after the First World War. And their industrial interests were mo more confined to textiles alone as was the case with the large majority of the nineteenth century entrepreneurs. They also entered sugar, cement, starch, construction, newspapers and publishing, banking, insurance, and a host of other minor industries. The industrial base of the country was still narrow which provided but limited scope for input industries such as chemicals to develop. But what is important is that as a result of the developments during the two world wars, the Indian industrial scene became much more variegated both in terms of manufacturing interests as well as the social composition of emerging business class.

The most spectacular development was the entry of the Marwaris into the modern sector. Comprising emigres of varied social backgrounds from Rajasthan—although taking their name from Marwar from where the first group moved out in search of better opportunities than that arid zone could provide—they were engaged primarily in trading, money-lending, brokerage, and speculation in practically every part of the country almost up to the end of the First World War. Although we do find a few stray instances of Marwaris acquiring financial interests in a few Bombay cotton mills in the last quarter of the nineteenth century, their entry into modern industries in a real sense did not begin until shortly before the war ended, The process of transition started in Bengal, particularly Calcutta, where the Marwaris had the most emphatic presence. By the turn of the century, their dominance on the internal trade in raw jute was almost complete and they also had sizeable share in exports.[30] Using the capital accumulated through these operations, they took two principal routes or a combination of both to modern industries: (i) acquiring sizeable shares in companies controlled by others, mostly expatriate firms, through stock market operations and (ii) buying off units already in existence or setting up new companies of their own.

Through these methods they made deep inroads into the areas dominated until then by European interests, viz., jute and coal mining, Cotton textiles was another favourite field, and when sugar was granted protection in 1930, many Marwaris established sugar mills. Some of the best known Calcutta-based Marwari families that entered modern industries after the war included the Birlas, Bangurs, Poddars, Kanorias, Somanis, and Jalans. The enterprises set up by them, however, were not confined to the city of their adoption; they were located in several parts of the country. Marwaris residing in other regions too appeared on the industrial scene during the period between the two world wars. The Bajajs, Dalmias, Ruias, Kamanis and Piramals in Bombay, Seksarias and Bhandaris in central India, Jaipurias in Delhi, Khaitans and Singhanias in the United Provinces (now Uttar Pradesh) and Raigarhias in Bihar are but a few examples. With the exception of the jute mills and collieries, which had to be located in or around Bengal region because of locational advantages, most of the early Marwari enterprises were set up in regions where modern industries had made little progress till then such as the United Provinces (Kanpur and Deoria-Gorakhpur), Central India (Indore, Gwalior, Ujjain, Jabalpur, Delhi) and even Deccan (Hyderabad).[31]

Ghanshyamdas Birla and his family symbolize more than any other single Marwari the transition of his community from trade to industry, and a brief account of his business career may illustrate the process.[32] Maheshwari Bania by caste, the Birlas originated from Pilani in Rajasthan. The family, seeking better commercial opportunities, moved to Bombay shortly after the rebellion of 1857 and made a small fortune during the speculation mania generated by the American Civil War. Dealing in opium, silver, sugar and cotton, they established themselves comfortably in trade but decided to move to Calcutta when Bombay was threatened by plague around the turn of the century. Born in 1894 Ghanshyamdas was a young child then. The experience of the opium trade the Birlas had gained in Bombay stood then in good stead in Calcutta; their employment with the highly influential firm of Tarachand Ghanshyamdas during the first few years at Calcutta sharpened their skills still further. They also gained a good understanding of the jute and hessian markets. As their insights into the intricacies of the Calcutta business world increased, they left their employers and set up a firm of their own—Baldevdas Jugalkishore—after the names of Ghanshyamdas's father and elder brother respectively. By the time the First World War broke out, the Birlas had firmly established themselves in the Calcutta markets and their fortunes received a further boost with the war-time boom. According to a rough estimate, their total worth during these years rose almost four times—from Rs. 20 lakhs to Rs. 80 lakhs. And in this achievement, the role of Ghanshyamdas was considerable.

By this time Ghanshyamdas had also emerged as a prominent leader of an influential group of Marwaris who wanted the community to develop a modern, progressive outlook, shed off its traditional conservative image and develop closer links with the emerging forces of Indian nationalism. During the formative period of his commercial life, Ghanshyamdas had been subjected to overt racial discrimination by his English clients. At the same time, his business contact with them had also instilled in him a certain degree of grudging regard for 'their superiority in business methods, their organising capacity and their many other virtues'.[33] These experiences during the impressionable phase of his life seem to have left an indelible mark on his thinking process and continued to influence his business and political behaviour throughout his life.

Apart from the augmented financial power that came in the wake of the war, a sense of constructive indignation against the expatriate business interests could have been an important factor in Ghanshyamdas's decision to enter modern industries as early as in 1916 when he acquired a sick cotton mill in Delhi. That this was not an impulsive decision but the result of a conscious plan is clear from the fact that two years later, the Birlas formed their managing agency firm, the Birla Brothers, which would be responsible for the management of their industrial establishments. However, perhaps their most momentous decision was to establish the Birla Jute Mill in Calcutta in blatant defiance of the Scottish monopoly. Another cotton mill, Jiyajeerao Cotton at Gwalior was added in 1921 and Kesoram Cotton was purchased from Andrew Yule & Co., a British managing agency firm, in 1928. The same year a confectionery unit, owned earlier by an expatriate firm, was brought under the Birla fold. In the meantime, the Birlas had also gone into publishing and soap and chemicals, though in a modest way. And within three years of sugar being granted protection by the Indian Tariff Board, they had opened four sugar mills in the

United Provinces and Bihar. By the middle of the 1930s, they also had an insurance firm and a paper company under their control. All this created a good base for taking effective steps towards new lines when the Second World War provided a new stimulant for growth—textile machinery manufacture, automobiles, bicycles, non-ferrous metals, vegetable oil, rayon and banking.

Birla's resentment against the foreign domination of Indian industries was also reflected in his move to form an Indian trade association, independent of the Associated Chambers of Commerce controlled then by European interests. As the gulf between the Indian and European interests had been widening for some time, his initiative received a ready response from a large section of the Indian business, resulting in the birth of the Federation of Indian Chambers of Commerce and Industry in 1927.[34] By this time, Ghanshyamdas had also been drawn much closer to the nationalist moment—particularly Gandhi, its undisputed leader.

All Marwaris, of course, did not share Birla's attitude to the nationalist movement or European business nor did all of them follow the same route to modern industries. But most of those who, like Birla were among the first to establish or acquire industrial enterprises sympathized with his progressive outlook and reformist zeal for his community; some others followed suit under the impact of the demonstration effect of the industrial success of the early entrants. The Marwaris still clinging to the conventional social norms and mores continued with their traditional pursuits. The maximum that they did was to acquire some interests in the enterprises controlled by expatriate firms through stock market operations and thus earn the right to be represented on the boards of these companies. A large majority of the Marwaris belonged to this category with the result that the community's presence on the industrial front was still rather modest when India became independent. Even the Birlas, the largest of them all, had less than twenty industrial firms (the number would go up to more than 150 within two and half decades after independence).[35]

The First World War did not have the same effect on the Chettiars as on the Marwaris. Though small in number, the community was concentrated mainly in the Madras region and had 'a reputation throughout the land for their spirit of adventure and enterprise, for their natural shrewdness and ability and for their acts of munificence'.[36] They had accumulated enormous capital through trading and moneylending in Burma, Malaya, and Indo-China from around the middle of the nineteenth century. However, as the business opportunities in southern India remained much more limited than in western and eastern India, the Chettiar traders and moneylenders continued to thrive in the relatively placid environment of the South-East Asian market where few were in a position to challenge their supremacy. Around the turn of the century, a very small part of the Chettiar capital began to be invested in minor industrial ventures in the Madras Presidency, but all that stood as the symbol of their interest in modern sectors in their own homeland at the outset of the war were three cotton mills, one sugar factory, a rice mill, two jute and cotton companies, and one bank.

This record compared favourably with that of the Marwaris in east and north India at this time, but the surprising fact is that the Chettiars showed little inclination to expand their industrial presence during or even after the war. The development of the Coimbatore textile industry, which started taking shape around the beginning of the second decade of the twentieth century, was the handiwork of Naidu or Kamma entrepreneurs, representing land holding communities. They first set up a large number of ginning units and then promoted a number of cotton mills in the immediate post-war years. The major role in this development was played by three Naidu families—G. Kuppuswami Naidu, V. Rangaswami Naidu and P.S.G. Naidu. They were all large landholders and had moved from the cultivation of cotton to cotton trading around the turn of the century. The profits made during the war years enabled them to develop Coimbatore as the most important textile centre in south India. Two or three Chettiar-promoted mills did come into existence between 1921 and 1925, but it was not until after 1930 that Chettiars began to look upon modern industry as an avenue of prudent investment in their homeland. The most important reason for this shift was the colossal losses the Chettiar moneylenders suffered in Burma around this time. The bulk of their funds, loaned on the security of agricultural land, became unrecoverable owing to the depression of 1930.[37] The Chettiars would overcome this shock and would emerge as the single most dominant caste group in the industrial life of south India, but at the time of independence, they were still busy reorganizing themselves to face the challenge of transition to industry. All that they had to signify their status as industrialists were a few cotton mills in the Madurai region.

In contrast, the non-commercial ethnic groups were much more visible on the industrial horizon of south India before independence.[38] We have already alluded to the role of the Naidus in developing the Coimbatore cotton industry. One of the most prominent industrial houses that emerged in south India between the two world wars was the outcome of the enterprising endeavours of the Seshasayee Brothers. Brahmin by caste and trained as electrical engineers, they started off with a road transport service around Trichinopoly (now Tiruchirapalli) in the Madras Presidency. They later moved into servicing and sale of buses, cars and motor cycles and then into design, supply and erection of electrical installations in south Madras during the early 1920s. By 1940, they were strong and solvent enough to take over the control of Mettur Chemical and Industrial Corporation. The most daring example of their entrepreneurial spirit, however, was the Fertilizers and Chemicals Travancore Ltd. Established in 1943, when fertilizer production had hardly begun in the country, this would grow into a most reputable concern soon after independence.

Another Brahmin entrepreneur who emerged in south India during the period was C. Rajan Iyer. Around the First World War he started trading in steel through his India Trading Company Ltd. Having improved his financial position and gained some experience of business in this line, he moved into industry with the promotion of Indian Steel Rolling Mills Ltd. in 1934. The genesis of what would emerge as the most prestigious industrial house in south India after independence, the T.V.S. Group, also goes back to the inter-war years. Its founder, T.V. Sundaram Iyengar, belonging to one of the most forward looking Brahman castes albeit sticking to a conventional life-style, started his business career with trading in timber in a small way and then moved to road transport shortly before the First World War. During the early 1920s, he included imported motor parts in his trading activities; by the end of the decade, however, he had acquired the sole selling agency of the products of General Motors, the American automobile giant. Through the sale and servicing of imported cars and motor parts, the Sundarams improved their resources so considerably that soon after independence, they were able to launch into modern industries in a big way, using their family firm T.V.S. and Sons Private Limited as the nucleus.

The number of persons belonging to non-mercantile sections or without business background continued to increase in other parts of India as well. Even the Bengalis who had remained, with only rare exceptions, almost indifferent to business after the disappointing experience of the 1840s, were lured to try their luck, and at least half a dozen enterprises owned and managed by Bengalis of diverse social origins existed when the First World War broke out. They had come into being under the impact of the Swadeshi movement and did not last long. Gujaratis of all social backgrounds started a host of firms in a variety of lines, the Patidars, traditionally a landholding agricultural community, being the most conspicuous among the newcomers. The entry of Punjabi Khatris, who trace their decent from the ancient Kshatriyas, into the modern sector was heralded by Karam Chand Thapar, belonging to Ludhiana. His father, a small landholder, would have liked him to join the police service but the young man, having failed in his B.A. examination, moved to Calcutta with a family friend where he started trading in coal in the early 1920s. Within less than a decade he was sufficiently prosperous to acquire a sugar mill in the United Provinces and a little later to go into paper manufacturing. Shortly before independence he had also brought a textile mill under his control. Another Khatri family, the Mahindras, had also taken the first firm steps toward becoming the pioneers of jeep production in India. A Sikh, Indra Singh, also emerged as an industrialist around the same time with a number of enterprises in engineering and textile.[39]

In the meantime, most of the enterprises set up earlier by persons of non-mercantile origins continued to prosper and grow. Martin Burn & Co. under the leadership of Rajendra Nath Mookerjee emerged as one of the most reputable engineering firms in the entire country. Ray's Bengal Chemicals did not make much progress but remained respectable. The Kirloskars expanded several fold, producing a variety of sophisticated engineering goods such as oil engines, machine tools and electric motors and generators. The Alembic Chemical Works, despite many adverse factors, achieved some degree of stability during the inter-war years, paving the ground for the rise of the respectable Amin Group later. A more prominent Patidars house that came to its own during this period was that of the Mafatlals. Starting their industrial career with the establishment of a textile mill in Ahmedabad in 1905, the Mafatlals later moved to Bombay and diversified into jute, sugar, shipping and plywood during the 1930s and 40s.[40]

The older business groups, controlled by the so-called commercial castes, demonstrated similar trends during the two world wars as those owned by persons of non-commercial origin, Tata's steel company, despite facing difficult times during the mid-1920s, finally stabilized itself and the house moved into some of the most challening fields—hydro-electric power, chemicals, civil aviation, and heavy vehicles along with the manufacture of some consumer items. The Birlas, despite their impressive record of expansion, were still not in a position to threaten the Tatas' pre-eminence and continued to occupy a distant second place in the Indian industrial world. The progress of enterprises set up by Walchand Hirachand, a Sholapur-based Jain of Gujarati origin, remained uneven. His construction companies and agro-business units prospered, but his most prestigious undertaking, the Scindia Steamship Navigation Co., continued to have a precarious existence, and some of his other ambitious projects like shipbuilding, aircraft manufacturing and passenger car production remained either stillborn or made slow progress. And while most of the textile-based houses of Bombay and Ahmedabad demonstrated limited propensity for diversification, the Delhi Cloth Mills under the leadership of Lala Shri Ram emerged as the most diversified enterprise of its kind with controlling interests in sugar, sewing machines, electric fans and potteries.[41]

III

What this survey indicates is that the industrial transition of India cannot be attributed to the efforts of a few selected religious-cultural collectivities, often called business communities. On the contrary, right from the beginning of the process of industrialization around the middle of the nineteenth century, persons cutting across caste and community boundaries but influenced by certain set of forces promoted and nursed industrial opportunities all over the country. Neither the progress, resilience and expansion nor the failure, vulnerability and contraction of these enterprises were contingent on the soci-cultural origin of the entrepreneur. In fact, almost half of the major business houses at the time of India's independence had been promoted and developed by people who had no previous experience of business and claimed no affiliation to the so-called business castes.[42] What is even more significant is the fact that all of them had more or less similar approaches to organizational structures and functional strategies. At any rate, variations, if any, had little to do with the socio-cultural backgrounds of those who controlled these enterprises.

The forms of ownership and managerial structure under which the Indian enterprises developed offer the best example of this. When the Indians embarked upon the industrial course, most of the British textile companies were partnership firms and continued to be so well up to the First World War.[43] In contrast, Davar's mill, the very first founded in India, had several features usually associated with a joint stock concern. It was not a full-fledged joint stock company but, with more than fifty shareholders with limited liability, it was not exactly a partnership either. A historian of the Bombay textile industry has called it a 'co-partnerships'. To appreciate the full significance of this experiment, it is necessary to recall that the joint stock principle was barely known in India then and the Indian Companies Act, passed barely four years before this company was launched, provided no legal support to the limited liability principle. As this disability was removed by an amendment in 1857, most of the future industrial firms established by the Indians were organized as joint stocks with limited liabilities. Surprisingly, the textile firms in Britain continued to adhere to the partnership pattern even though the limited liability principle had been incorporated in British law a year before it was adopted in India.[44]

Why the English manufacturers chose to cling to the older form of ownership even after the legislation of 1856 is not our concern. Nor is it easy to discern the motive behind the adoption of the joint stock system by the Indian entrepreneurs. Perhaps the partnership pattern was too deeply entrenched in England to be easily disturbed merely by legislative changes. And it is possible that the Indian pioneers, unencumbered by any indigenous precedence of the ownership pattern in large factory establishments, found it easier to embrace a system which had the potential to attract small investors. With their limited resources, such investors would have been unable or unwilling to join a partnership. That they did not come forward at the initial stages to acquire shares in the joint stock textile companies is beside the point. It is well known that early promoters distributed the shares of their concerns among their own close relatives and friends. But what is pertinent is that the pioneers might have calculated that once their manufacturing enterprises would get consolidated, the initially cautious and hesitant parties would feel encouraged to join their capital structure. At later stages of the development of Indian industry, a number of cotton companies in fact did dilute the family holdings of the promoters in their share capital.

Embarking on the joint stock system rather than the partnership so successfully tested by the British producers was, thus, an act of some foresight on the part of Indian pioneers. It was also consistent with the Indian environment in which both capital and managerial ability were scarce. While the textile manufacturers gave the lead, the promoters of industrial companies in other fields also adopted the joint stock concept for their own purposes and, thus, established its viability as an instrument of industricalization. Being a purely indigenous development rather than an emulation of British practices, it must be regarded as an organizational innovation consistent with Indian conditions and realities.

The Indian approach to management structure also differed radically from that in vogue in Great Britain when the Indians started moving into modern industries. While the Lancashire mills were managed by salaried managing directors who worked under the overall control of boards of directors, the Indian pioneers, in contrast. adopted for their purpose a structure almost unique to India. Whatever the origin, the managing agency system of corporate management under which the Indian industries developed, was yet to establish itself when the early Indian pioneers embarked on textile ventures. Thus, without any meaningful precedence, whether in India or abroad, the adoption of the new form of management involved some degree of risk and required a great deal of imagination.

The *modus operandi* was simple. A family with considerable financial strength would launch a company and allot to its own members or near relatives and close friends sufficient number of shares necessary to control the new concern. The management of this concern would be entrusted on a long-term basis to a family firm of the promoters. Though this was done through a resolution of the shareholders, it was a mere formality in view of the promoters holding controlling interests. The firms to which the management of industrial concerns was entrusted in this manner were called managing agencies, and these usually were partnerships of the family members or sole proprietorships. Under this arrangement, it is obvious, the role of the head of the promoting family in directing the affairs of the managing agency, and therefore of the industrial companies entrusted to its care, was in no way different from his role in managing his family in other spheres. A managing agency for all practical purposes, thus, was an organizational fiction, an euphemism for family control. Technically, the managing agents did not own the companies, but in practice it was they who took all critical and strategic decisions. The boards of directors, constituted to satisfy legal requirements, were no more than mere rubber-stamping decorations, as their members were hand-picked by the managing agents themselves.

The Indian pioneers of textile ventures were the first to experiment with the managing agency system. The structure adopted for Davar's cotton company, as has been said earlier, anticipated many essential features of the system which developed fully in subsequent years and embraced practically the entire Indian corporate world. J.N. Tata did try to emulate the British system of salaried managing director in his Empress Mill, but had to revert to the Indian system barely after two years of experience.[45]

The development of the managing agency system has been attributed to 'the peculier circumstances prevailing in India'.[46] Among the factors often considered responsible for its origin and gradual evolution was the scarcity of capital and managerial ability.[47] Sociological reasons, however, were no less significant. Shorn of details, the managing agency framework represented an adaptation of the joint family system, still a prominent feature of the Indian social structure, to the industrial situation. The head of a joint family controlled the purse, exercised authority over the junior members, and had a dominant, almost decisive, voice in almost everything that concerned the family. All families, whether they were involved in business or some other occupation, were managed in this fashion. The business management structure, thus, was coterminous with the family management structure.

The managing agency system meant no departure from this

structure and entailed little or no threat to the authority of the head in managing the industrial concerns floated by the family. It is this social reality more than anything else that led to its universal acceptance in India and its continuance for almost a century. True, the system was open to abuses, and some managing agents actually did misuse their powers and privileges, but whether any other organizational structure would have been more effective in the Indian milieu of the times is doubtful indeed.[48]

Proprietary concerns and partnerships continued to exist in large numbers throughout this period, and these of course remained out of the managing agency fold. It is possible that most of these firms were owned by families with commercial background, who did not have to depend on outside investment because of their own financial resources. It is also possible that finance even for their joint stock companies came from people belonging to their own class, thanks to their social and business linikages and relatively undeveloped state of stock markets, while new entrants into industries, without previous commercial background, had to depend on widely dispersed and much larger number of investors. However, the fact that a large majority of registered firms for which data are available were joint stock concerns[49] and only a very small percentage of such enterprises remained out of the managing agency umbrella would indicate that both these categories of company promoters followed essentially similar strategies for raising industrial finance and organizing their industrial enterprises—variations being more the result of their respective situations than of basic approach. And all industrial concerns, regardless of the social origins of the controlling families, followed similar marketing strategies: all of them depended on commission agents and other established channels to market their products almost up to the onset of independence.

Also, the variations in social origin and other respects made little difference to their approach to choice and development of technology. They all emulated, blindly and uncritically, Western practices, particularly those prevailing in Great Britain in this regard. This can be attributed to three major factors. First, India had had no technological tradition worth the name before the beginning of factory industry in the country and thus most Indian entrepreneurs had very little insights into technological matters. Second, when the process of industrial transition in India started,

Great Britain was the most dominant industrial power in the world. The Indians naturally looked at the metropolitan country as the principal source of industrial machinery and technical manpower, and for them the guidance of British machinery manufacturers in the choice of technology and production devices had an aura of finality about it. The progress of industrialization in other Western countries, challenging British supremacy in this sphere, and the introduction of technical education in India in later years made little difference in the situation. For, Indians had much greater exposure to the glittering economic might of Great Britain, and the progress of technical education in India remained slow both in quantitative and qualitative terms. And finally, the preference for quick profit, inherited from pre-industrial days, remained an overriding concern with the management of Indian enterprises.

It was not only the entrepreneurs belonging to the relatively less progressive mercantile classes who continued to be guided by this consideration; others too, despite their educational background and more enlightened outlook, could not disregard it for fear of jeopardizing their competitive capacity and thus the future of their enterprises. The non-business background of the latter group of entrepreneurs was sufficient to create doubt about their competence to manage a business enterprise. The failure of their companies to yield returns comparable to commercial undertakings or industrial enterprises set up by more experienced commercial interests would have only reinforced this doubt. All this not only placed an unwarranted, though understandable, limit on the Indians' choice of technology but also inhibited experimentation to modify the borrowed technology to suit Indian conditions and need. The colonial syndrome and liquidity preference, thus, generated a sort of technological myopia, as it were, among the Indian promoters of industry.

The attitude to textile technologies in India would illustrate this point. Take for, instance, the ring spindles. Although Tata's Empress Mills had introduced this spinning device developed in the United States as early as 1883 and demonstrated that it was better suited to Indian labour conditions and product lines of most Indian mills at that time, the diffusion of the ring technology remained much slower in India than in Japan. It has been argued that the Indian preference was due to the capability of mule to spin finer counts, but this view can hardly be sustained in the face of the fact that almost up to the end of the First World War, most mills concentrated on the production of coarse yarn. The only explanation for the slow diffusion of ring system in India is that it was adopted very slowly in Great Britain. The popularity graph of the ring frame started going up in England only after the First World War and it was only after 1920 that the real spurt in the use of the ring occurred in India by which time mule had practically disappeared from the Japanese factories.[50]

The Indian millowners also paid little heed to another experiment which the Japanese exploited with great deal of profit: blending of various varieties of cotton wool. The Indians must have known of the European experiment in this regard during the cotton crisis of 1861—after all it was the Indian cotton that was mixed with the available superior variety[51]—but if they remained insensitive to its benefit, perhaps the only plausible explanation is that the practice was never adopted in the British mills. Adoption of the mixing method would have helped the Indians to produce better quality of coarse goods than the Indian staple by itself was capable of yielding, and reduce at the same time the production cost of the superior count. Also the diffusion of the ring process would have been easier, for the presence of superior cotton in the blend would have neutralized a supposed advantage of mule which, it was believed rightly or wrongly, worked better with the Indian variety.

The adoption of these devices, as we have seen, were among the major factors that enabled Japan to challenge India's supremacy in East Asian markets by the mid-1890s and eventually force its giant competitor out of these regions by 1913. Worse still, Japan began to make inroads into India's domestic market as well. The First World War temporarily halted the Japanese assault, but the danger assumed an alarming character around the early 1920s because of the price advantages the Japanese textile goods enjoyed in India despite heavy tariffs. This was, to a large extent, due to the Indian producers' indifference to the benefits of automatic power loom, which could greatly reduce the labour cost. While the use of this device in Japan became fairly general within two decades after it had been perfected—and Japan in fact had developed its own automatic powerloom by the mid-1920s, as we have seen earlier—

in India ordinary looms constituted almost 98 per cent of all looms in India as late as 1934.[52] We have no other explanation for the Indian indifference to this labour-saving technology except that, since it was considered unsuitable for most of the specialized products of the British mills, it never became popular in Great Britain.

If the ability of the Indian textile producers to evaluate the relative benefits of the available technologies was so befogged by the colonial syndrome, it was a forgone conclusion that they would depend on foreign technical personnel much longer than necessary, and that they would do precious little to modify the imported technology or invest in developing indigenous devices. What is, however, more significant is that the technological approaches of the promoters of the industries that started taking shape in the first half of the twentieth century too bears little evidence that India was developing any great sense of technological autonomy. The only difference was that unlike the textile producers, they did not look at Britain alone as the source of technology. As for modifying the imported technology or attempting to develop indigenous devices to suit Indian conditions, their record is no better.

Let us take the case of Tatas, perhaps the most progressive of and enterprising of all business houses, to illustrate this point. Their founder, we may recall, was the first Indian textile producer to appreciate the relative advantages of the ring frame. Their cotton mills in later period, however, were as slow in embracing new technological devices, such as automatic power looms, as others. Also, even though they did perceive industrial opportunities in areas involving a great deal of risk, heavy investment and long gestation period, and the technologies for these projects were selected with great deal of care, Tatas' entrepreneurship never extended to research and development conducive to technological innovations. It is possible that their growing pre-occupation with the heavy industries enterprises in the present century prevented them from giving adequate attention to the technological aspects of their textile operations, and their hydro-electric and heavy vehicle related projects were still too young to permit meaningful technological experimentation, but even their flagship concern TISCO had little to offer by way of proof of its technological autonomy.

A few facts would bear this out. The company understandably had to depend on foreign technical personnel initially, but such dependence continued for a long time. The first concrete step to develop technical expertise of the Indian staff was not taken until 1921 when the Jamshedpur Technical Institute was set up, and an apprentic school to develop trained operatives came into being only in 1927. The process of Indianising the works, however, did not begin until 1931, the first Indian general manager did not take over until 1938, and the company still had some foreign experts occupying senior posts as late as in 1944. Under these conditions, the question of any significant modification in the processes did not arise. In fact, every time the TISCO diversified into new product lines, it turned to foreign, usually British, companies for collaboration.[53] Even more revealing of the Tatas' indifference to technological aspects is the fact that practically no attempt was made to increase the efficiency of the production system with a view to reducing costs per unit of output or improve quality for given cost. The result was that the changes in production function via technical progress contributed little to TISCO's rate of growth.[54]

The record of companies engaged in the production of goods requiring technologies much less intricate, such as cement, sugar, starch and chemicals, is no better, and the attitude of the entrepreneurs with personal command over appropriate technical expertise, i.e. Kirloskars, P.C. Ray, Seshasayees, was no different. Political sympathies did not make much dent on the technological-inertia either, as Walchand, Kirloskar or Birla with all their nationalistic leanings continued, as others did, to depend on imported technology with no attempt even at process innovation. It is no surprise that under these conditions the number of Indian applications for patents remained negligible. As late as in 1930, out of a total of 1099 applications filed in Indian patent offices, only 212 originated in India, less than 4 per cent of the number in Japan around the same time; the rest were from Europeans. And most of these 212 related to agricultural implements, irrigation equipment or other simple devices centered around craftsmanship.[55]

To sum up this discussion, there is no question that the Indian entrepreneurial scenario underwent a sea-change between the establishment of India's first industrial venture and the end of colonial rule. In the wake of the infrastructural development consequent upon the growing political integration, a national market, covering the entire length and breadth of the country had emerged and many roablocks—tight grip of dogmas and traditions on occupational choices, religious-cultural inhibitions against business activities, age-old occupational impobility, and even the liquidity preference of the mercantile classes—had been either dismantled or were being pushed aside. In other words, the environmental changes that were still at the nascent stage around the middle of the nineteenth century consolidated themselves considerably during the next hundred years.

All this naturally expanded the horizon of perceivable business opportunities both quantitatively and qualitatively. This was reflected in an increasingly larger number of people, drawn from diverse socio-cultural groups, perceiving and exploiting industrial opportunities. Their approaches to strategies and structures were essentially similar, and they exhibited a growing tendency for joining hands with one another to safeguard their common business interests, despite socio-cultural diversities. In other words, an Indian business class held together by a community of economic interests was definitely taking shape when India became free.

However, unlike Japan which was fully ripe for industrial transformation when its first industrial enterprise was set up, the environmental forces conducive to rapid transition were still at an embryonic stage in India when the factory system made its appearance in the country. Industrial opportunities could have been only hazily perceived, and timidly exploited under these conditions. This hurt the Indian experiment in two ways: (i) it gave India a much slower start and (ii) the kind of mutual reinforcement that a more favourable constellation of forces and the resultant bolder entrepreneurial response can offer to each other was denied to it. This naturally affected the pace of change and the process of consolidation in respect of both remained understandably slow all through the period under review.

Under these conditions, it is not at all surprising that the 'take off' stage, which Japan reached within about three decades of launching its first textile mill, was nowhere in sight for India when the country became free—even after almost a century of the birth of its first industrial enterprise.

NOTES

1. Blair B. Kling, *Partner in Empire: Dwarkanath Tagore and the Age of Enterprise in Eastern India* (Berkeley: University of California Press, 1976), pp. 243-5.
2. Morris D. Morris, 'The Growth of Large-Scale Industry to 1948, in *The Cambridge Economic History of India, Vol. II, c. 1757-c. 1970*, ed. by Dharma Kumar (Cambridge: Cambridge University Press, 1982), pp. 566-7.
3. Ibid., pp. 574-5.
4. S.D. Mehta, *Cotton Mills of India, 1854-1954* (Bombay: Textile Association, 1954), pp. 3-63.
5. F.R. Harris, *Jamsetji Nusserwanji Tata: A Chronicle of His Life* (London: Blackie & Son, 1958), pp. 146-218.
6. E.E. Hagen in his *On the Theory of Social Change: How Economic Growth Begins* (Homewood, Ill.: Dorsey Press, 1962), has suggested this hypothesis on the basis of his analysis of situation in Burma (pp. 468-70), although he finds the Indian situation too complex (pp. 427-8).
7. In a letter to *The Times of India*, J.N. Tata alluded to this distinctness by referring to non-Parsee Indians as 'Pure natives'. Quoted in Dwijendra Tripathi and M. Mehta, *Business Houses in Western India: A Study in Entrepreneurial Response* (New Delhi: Manohar, 1990), p. 71.
8. Ibid., pp. 37-54; see also Bhagwanlal R. Badshah, *Rao Bahadur Ranchhodlal Chhotalal C.I.E.* (Ahmedabad: Aryodaya Press, 1899); S.M. Edwardes, *Memoir of Rao Bahadur Ranchhodlal Chhotalal C.I.E.* (Exter: William Pollard & Co., 1920); Howard Spodek, 'Manchesterization of Ahmedabad', *Economic Weekly*, Vol. 17, No. 11 (13 March 1965).
9. For details, see Amlendu Guha, 'Comprador Role of Parsi Sheths, 1750-1850', *Economic and Political Weekly*, Vol. 5, No. 8 (28 Nov. 1970); and 'More About the Parsi Sheths: Their Roots, Entrepreneurship and Comprador Role, 1650-1918' in *Business Communities of India*, ed. by Dwijendra Tripathi (New Delhi: Manohar, 1984), pp. 109-150.
10. Tripathi and Mehta, *Business Houses . . .*, p. 50.
11. Ibid., pp. 76-87.
12. Natwarlal N. Parikh, *Directory of Ahmedabad Mill Industry, 1929-1955* (Ahmedabad: N.N. Parikh, 1958), pp. 38-41.
13. Harris, *Tata . . .*, pp. 23-63.
14. Tripathi and Mehta, *Business Houses . . .*, p. 47.
15. Morris, 'The Growth of Large-Scale Industry . . .', pp. 580-1.

16. Tripathi and Mehta, *Business Houses . . .* , pp. 44-6; also, Spodex, 'Manchesterization . . .', passim.
17. Of the 95 mills established in Bombay before 1914, Parsees promoted 34, Hindus 27, Europeans 15, Muslims 10 and Jews 5, with classification of 4 not being clear (Morris, 'Growth of Large-Scale Industry . . .', p. 580; while in Ahmedabad Vaishnava Banias and Jains together controlled 41 out of the 53 mills in 1914. Dwijendra Tripathi, 'Birth, Growth and Death of Firms in a Proto-Industrial Economy: The Experience of the Ahmedabad Textile Industry, 1858-1929', *Indian Historical Review*, Vol. 16, Nos. 1-2 (July 1989 and Jan. 1990); Desai, *Directory . . .* , passim.
18. Although 6 large cotton mills had been established in Kanpur between 1861 and 1923, they were all in European hands. The Indians entered the field only after the First World War. H. Fukuzawa, 'Cotton Mills Industry' in V.B. Singh, *Economic History of India* (Bombay: Allied Publishers, 1965), pp. 230-1.
19. Arun Joshi, *Lala Shri Ram: A Study in Entrepreneurship and Industrial Management* (New Delhi: Orient Longman, 1975), pp. 37-70.
20. K.P. Thomas, 'The History of the House of Martin Burn', *Homma's Annual of Calcutta* (Calcutta: K.P. Thomas, 1953).
21. Tripathi and Mehta, *Business Houses . . .* , p. 117.
22. Ibid., pp. 116-30.
23. Ibid., pp. 131-46.
24. For critical evaluation of *laissez faire* in India, see S. Bhattacharya, 'Laissez Fair in India', *Indian Economic and Social History Review*, Vol. 2, No. 1 (Jan. 1965); Dwijendra Tripathi, 'Opportunism of Free Trade: Lancashire Cotton Famine and Indian Cotton Cultivation', *Indian Economic and Social History Review*, Vol. 4, No. 3 (Sept. 1967); idem, 'Opportunism of Free Trade: Sadasheogarh Harbour Project, 1855-1865', *Indian Economic and Social History Review*, Vol. 5, No. 4 (Dec. 1965).
25. Mehta, *Cotton Mills . . .* , pp. 34-85; see also K.N. Chaudhuri, 'Foreign Trade and Balance of Payments (1757-1947)' in *Cambridge Economic History of India . . .* , Vol. II, pp. 865-9.
26. Thomas A. Timberg, *The Marwaris from Traders to Industrialists* (New Delhi: Vikas, 1980), pp. 41-62; Shoji Ito, 'A Note on the "Business Combine" in India—with Special reference to the Nattukottai Chettiers', *Developing Economies*, Vol. 4, No. 3 (Sept. 1966).
27. Mehta, *Cotton Mills . . .* , pp. 86-99; Elwin, Verrier, *The Story of Tata Steel* (Bombay: Tata Sons Ltd., 1958).
28. Dwijendra Tripathi, 'Congress and the Indian Industrialists (1885-1947)' in *Business and Politics in India*, ed. by Dwijendra Tripathi (New Delhi: Manohar, 1991), pp. 86-123.

29. Dwijendra Tripathi, 'The Silver Question: India and America', *Journal of Indian History*, Vol., 44, No. 132 (Sept. 1967), pp. 255-63.
30. Omkar Goswami, 'Then Came the Marwaris: Some Aspects of the Changes in the Pattern of Industrial Control in Eastern India', *Indian Economic and Social History Review*, Vol. 22, No. 3 (Oct.-Dec. 1985).
31. Timberg, *The Marwaris* . . . , pp. 180-228.
32. Gita Piramal and M. Herdeck, *India's Industrialists* (Washington, D.C.: Three Continents Press, 1985), pp. 59-103; see also Ram Niwas Jaju, *G.D. Birla: A Biography* (New Delhi: Vikas, 1985).
33. G.D. Birla, *In the Shadow of the Mahatma* (Bombay: Orient Longman, 1955), p. xv.
34. Stanley Kochanek, *Business and Politics in India* (Berkeley: University of California Press), pp. 108-30; see also H. Venkatasubbiah, *Enterprise and Economic Change: 50 years of FICCI* (New Delhi: Vikas, 1977); Dwijendra Tripathi, 'From Community to Class: The Marwari in Historical Perspective' in *The Marwaris of Calcutta: Economic Times Special Feature*, 30 April 1988, pp. 3-11.
35. Goswami, 'Then Came the Marwaris . . . , pp. 230-5; Timberg, *The Marwaris* . . . , p. 197.
36. L.C. Jain, *Indigenous Banking in India* (London: Macmillan, 1929), p. 30.
37. This account of the Chettiars is based on Shoji Ito, 'A Note on the Business Combine in India . . . , and Raman Mahadevan, 'Entrepreneurship and Business Communities in Colonial Madras, 1900-1929', in *Business Communities of India: A Historical Perspective*, ed. by Dwijendra Tripathi (New Delhi: Manohar, 1984), pp. 225-39.
38. Mahadevan, 'Entrepreneurship and Business Communities . . .', see also Raman Mahadevan, 'Some Aspects of Pattern of Industrial Investment and Entrepreneurship in Travancore during the 1930s and 1940s' presented at Seminar on 'South Indian Economy, *c.* 1914-*c.* 1945' at Centre for Development Studies: Trivandrum, 25-27 April 1988.
39. Bengali enterprises are discussed in Omkar Goswami, 'Sahibs, Babus and Banias: Changes in Industrial Control in Eastern India 1918-1960' presented at Seminar on 'Strategy and Structure in Indian Business: A Historical Perspective' held at the Indian Institute of Management, Ahmedabad, 6-8 April 1987; for others see, Piramal and Herdeck *India's Industrialists* . . . ; Tripathi and Mehta, *Business Houses* . . . ; R.K. Hazari, *The Structure of the Private Sector: A Study of Concentration, Ownership and Control* (Bombay: Asia Publishing House, 1966).

40. For details, see Thomas, 'The History . . .'; Tripathi and Mehta, *Business Houses* . . . , Chaps. 6, 7 and 8.
41. Tripathi and Mehta, *Business Houses*, Chaps. 3, 4 and 9; Joshi, *Lala Shri Ram* . . . .
42. Of the twenty largest business groups in India during the 1950s, according to Hazari, two—Bird Heilger and Andrew—were British in origin, and Juggimal Kamlapet, Bangurs, Shapoorji, Indra Singh, Ram Krishna and Mahindras became prominent only after Independence. In terms of the social background of the controlling families, the remaining fourteen were evenly split between business and non-business communities: Tata (Parsee), Birla (Marwari), Dalmia-Sahu Jain (Jain, the house broke up after independence), Shri Ram (Agrawal Bania), Kasturbhai and Walchand (both Jain) belonged to the first category while Martin Burn (Brahmin), Thapar (Khatri), Mafatlals (Patidar), Khatau (Bhatia) and Kirloskar and Seshasayees (both Brahmans) to the second. Both Khatris and Bhatias trace their descent from ancient Kshatriayas. Hazari, *The Structure* . . . .
43. Textile Institute, *Management in the Textile Industry* (Manchester: Textile Institute, 1969), p. 2.
44. Mehta, *Cotton Mills* . . . , p. 9; R.S. Rungta, *The Rise of Business Corporations in India, 1850-1900* (Cambridge: Combridge University Press, 1970), pp. 36-45 and 212-16.
45. Harris, *Jamsetji Nusserwanji Tata* . . . , p. 27.
46. Vera Anstey, *Economic Development of India* (Lodon: Longman's Green & Co., 1957), p. 113.
47. P.S. Loknathan, *Industrial Organization in India* (London: George Allen and Unwin, 1935), pp. 13-40; 213-33.
48. For a fuller discussion, see Dwijendra Tripathi, 'Innovations in the Indian Textile Industry: The Formative Years' in *The Textile Industry and Its Business Climate*, ed. by Akio Okochi and Shinichi Yonekawa (Tokyo: Tokyo University Press, 1982), pp. 175-93.
49. Rungta, *Business Corporations* . . . , pp. 46, 153, 298; S.S. Rutnagur (ed.), *Bombay Industries: The Cotton Mills* (Bombay: Bombay Textile Journal, 1927), pp. 97-243; also Tripathi, 'Innovations . . .', p. 178.
50. Gustav Ranis and Gary Saxonhouse, 'Determinants of Technology Choice: The Indian and Japanese Cotton Industries' in *Japan and Developing Countries: A Comparative Analysis*, ed. by Kazushi Ohkawa and Gustav Ranis (New York: Basil Blackwell, 1985), pp. 135-54; Gary Saxonhouse, 'Technology Choice in Cotton Textile Manufacturing' in ibid., pp. 212-35; Yukihiko Kiyokawa, 'Technical Adaptation and Managerial Resources in India: A Study

of the Experience of the Cotton Textile Industry from a Comparative Viewpoint', *Developing Economies*, Vol. 21, No. 2 (June 1983).

51. Dwijendra Tripathi, 'The United States and India: Economic Links, 1860-1900', Ph.D. Dissertation, University of Wisconsin, Madison, 1963, p. 70.
52. International Labour Organization, *The World Textile Industry: Economic and Social Problems* (Geneva: I.L.O., 1937), Vol. I, pp. 48-56; A.S. Pearse, *The Cotton Industry of India* (Manchester: International Federation of Master Cotton Spinners' and Manufacturers' Associations, 1930), p. 9; Binny Ltd., *The House of Binnys* (Madras: Binny Ltd., 1969), pp. 210-11. Interestingly the share of ordinary looms in the total number of looms in Great Britain was just about the same—97 per cent.
53. Tata Iron and Steel Co., *Tata Steel Diamond Jubilee 1907-67* (Jamshedpur: TISCO, 1967), pp. 23-74; Elwin, *The Story . . .*, pp. 68-70; see also R.K. Ray, *Industrialisation in India* (New Delhi: Oxford University Press, 1979), pp. 85-90.
54. P.N. Dhar and Omkar Seth, 'The Rate of Technical Progress in the Tata Iron and Steel Company in 1913-56', *Indian Economic Review*, Vol., 6 No. 1 (February 1962).
55. Morris, 'The Growth of Large-Scale Industry . . .', p. 639; Kiyokawa, 'Technical Adaptation . . .', p. 123. For a more comprehensive discussion on Indian technological choices, see Dwijendra Tripathi, 'Colonialism and Technology Choices in India: A Historical Overview', *Developing Economies*, Vol. 34, No. 1 (March 1996).

CHAPTER VI

Conclusion

THE PURPOSE OF a comparative analysis is to acquire a better comprehension of the phenomenon under focus. An understanding of the commonalities and variations in the experiences of two or more societies may provide insights which a country-specific study alone may not yield. What insights do we derive from comparing the experiences of Japan and India in a crucial area of human endeavour?

First, in both countries the rise of industrial entrepreneurship was preceded or accompanied by significant changes in the material environment and socio-cultural ethos. The quality and magnitude of these changes seem to have determined not only the quality and magnitude of entrepreneurial responses in these two countries but also the speed of industrial transformation. In Japan the stirrings of industrialization began after the stage had already been set for structural changes in the economy. In fact, it can be safely asserted that the preconditions for economic transition had attained such maturity in that country that the official restriction on the import of technology and occupational mobility were the only factors holding back the tide of entrepreneurial upsurge.

By removing these irksome restrictions and by reinforcing consciously and vigorously the positive trends in the environment, the Meiji authorities released the latent social energy to move the nation forward to the next logical economic stage. This is not to ignore the odious side of Tokugawa totalitarianism or berate the value of the Meiji contribution to the nation's industrial growth but only to emphasise that but for the previous developments, the post-Restoration order would have taken much longer and faced much greater hurdles to usher in the new industrial era.

The preconditions for industrial transition in India, on the other hand, were still at the nascent stage when the first cotton company was set up in Bombay. Quarreling for political control, the pre-British regimes of the country possessed neither the will nor the vision or power to generate forces which might have resulted in the expansion of the markets or otherwise minimized, to a reasonable degree, the risk of investment in large and unfamiliar ventures. It was only after the emergence of the British power on the Indian political firmament that these forces began to be generated, but they were yet to gain momentum or take firm roots when the first experiments in factory manufacturing commenced. In other words, the institutional arrangements existing in India around the middle of the nineteenth century were much less conducive to industrial transition than in Japan. As Morris D. Morris has suggested, in the context of the appropriateness of the prevailing socio-economic organization, the birth of the first cotton mills in India was more like the introduction of an economic novelty in the system rather than the beginning of a process of self-sustaining momentum.[1]

If India, in spite of obvious handicaps, preceded Japan in launching its industrial experiment by a few years, it was only because the governmental fiat did not impose an artificial limit on the former's freedom to acquire or use imported technology to which the country's colonial connection provided an easy access. However, since the Indians did not have the benefit of a meaningful technological tradition, their approach to technological choices and adaptation remained by and large static, while the Meiji Japan demonstrated a much more dynamic approach for which the technologists of the earlier era had prepared a solid ground. And yet, even the limited preconditions for change, developing during the British rule, opened up a new vista of industrial opportunities for increasingly larger number of Indians drawn from diverse social backgrounds. But in comparison with Japan, their number increased very gradually and their entrepreneurial manifestation remained rather limited because the pace and quality of industrialization process had to remain circumscribed by the parameters of institutional rearrangements, which evolved much more slowly in India than in Meiji Japan.

It is tempting to correlate the differential rate of expansion of institutional bases in the two countries in the latter half of the nineteenth century, to the character of their respective governments. There is no denying the fact that the colonial rulers of India exerted very little to generate the forces of industrial transition and left the matter entirely to the natural process of change, whereas the Meiji authorities attended to the task deliberately and with much greater vigour. It is worth remem-bering, however, that the environmental changes that had already occurred during the Tokugawa period must have had a multiplier effect on the Meiji measures directed to improving the climate for enterprise. In other words, a new constellation of forces, more conducive to economic breakthrough, was already emerging and had indeed been consolidated when the old order vanished. As Tapan Raychaudhari has pointed out, even though neither pre-Meiji Japan nor pre-British India was moving in the direction of spontaneous industrialization, Japan's 'society and economy more than those of pre-colonial India had the potentiality to respond to opportunities positively'.[2] The efforts of the post-Restoration government only reinforced the process.

India, in contrast, was exhibiting very feeble symptoms of dis-equilibrium between the existing institutional arrangements and economic opportunities and choices when the destiny of the country passed into the hands of an alien power. And the colonial government, true to its character, did precious little to consciously change the situation. However, if the preconditions for economic transition in British India were slow in developing, it was not only because of the inherent apathy of a colonial system in this regard but also because unlike Japan, the initial institutional base was woefully inadequate to sustain a faster improvement in the entrepreneurial climate. Under these conditions it is indeed doubtful that the process of change would have been more rapid even if the Mughals were followed by a native all-India power instead of the British.[3] In fact, the odds are that a better constellation of forces would have emerged even more haltingly.

Although the course of history cannot be made to re-run, speculation about possible alternatives available to a society can sometimes aid the understanding of historical processes. What would have happened if the Mughal hegemony had prevailed for another century is difficult to speculate about, but there can be no argument that the record of the successor regimes with respect to advancing the frontiers of economic opportunities, wittingly or otherwise, is almost dismal. Even the Marathas, the only native power capable of succeeding to the Mughal supremacy had not the British factor intervened, paid little heed to creating the basic minimum conditions for industrial transition in the territories under their control. Also, few princely states—those surviving relics of the old order—used the limited power and freedom, they still enjoyed within the Empire, to expand the horizon of economic choices and opportunities in their respective domains.[4]

The conclusion, thus, is inescapable that it was the British colonialism that sowed the seeds of such institutional changes without which industrial entrepreneurship could not have germinated.[5] This is not to gloss over the basically regressive character of the British colonialism. In fact, most positive changes in India were unintended by-products of the policies and programmes directed to tightening the imperial noose around the country's neck. But this in no way detracts from the fact that entrepreneurial climate in India improved significantly during the Raj although in most cases not because but in spite of it.

The British, thus, can be regarded as the first ever administrative system which cleared the ground, albeit unintendedly and insufficiently, for the rise of modern industries in India. In this respect their role in India was somewhat similar to that of the Tokugawas in Japan. Not only the institutional rearrangement underwent a radical transformation largely because of their imperial presence and interests but also a certain measure of industrial transition occurred, thanks to the new climate of enterprise created during their rule. In fact, the British left behind a more conducive constellation of forces for enterprise development than the Tokugawas bequeathed to the Meiji dispensation. And yet, the Indian economy after Independence took much longer to attain the 'take off'[6] than the Japanese economy after the Restoration.

An examination of this differential performance is beyond the purview of this study. It is possible that the Japanese success had something to do with the pursuit of a policy, which though essentially capitalistic, made for partnership between the government and private business, while the industrial policy of the post-colonial India was based on a basically adversarial relationship embedded in Western models.[7] Whatever the case, it is obvious that the political explanation for the differential economic performance of the two countries, centered around the character of their respective governments, need modification.

Our survey also rejects the cultural explanation of this phenomenon. For, the power of the socio-cultural ethos to block entrepreneurial evolution in both the societies was in direct proportion to the incapacity of material forces to expand the vistas of perceivable opportunities. And in both countries, religious inhibitions and value systems, sanctified by scriptures or traditions, were readapted or reinterpreted to facilitate the exploitation of new business opportunities that emerged in the wake of infrastructural changes. Even though the rituals remained intact, the behaviour changed significantly. This process in some respects seems to have been somewhat more rapid in British India, where there was no official injunction against occupational mobility or import of new technology, than in the Tokugawa Japan which looked upon these as unpartdonable heresies.

This is not to suggest, however, that the socio-cultural forces ceased to be a factor in the industrial life of these countries. The fact is that deep seated cultural values and social mores continued to permeate industrial concerns as much as the rest of the society in both the countries. The impact of group orientation, internal cohesion, and respect of hierarchy—the essential tenets of the Japanese social system—was no less evident on the structure and environment of the industrial organizations, than on the pre-Meiji commercial firms. Nor did the strategies adopted by the industrial establishments to achieve their business goal register a sharp break from the past. Similar was the case in India as well where the structural and strategic aspects of the business behaviour were marked by a remarkable degree of continuity, and whatever little changes occurred in these respects were quite consistent with the prevailing social realities. Industrial transition, it seems, can push its way through different socio-cultural parameters.

What does all this add up to our understanding of the process of industrial entrepreneurship in general? First, seen in a proper historical perspective, the stages of the growth of industrial entrepreneurship in different societies may manifest a greater degree of essential commonality than variation. Secondly, the understanding of these commonalities would require an integrated rather than a fragmented view of the factors generating forces of economic transition. Thirdly, political independence may be a necessary bat is not a sufficient condition for industrial change. And finally, the attempt to seek an explanation of economic behaviour of a people in prescribed socio-cultural norms alone may lead to misleading results.

NOTES

1. Morris D. Morris, 'The Growth of Large-Scale Industries' in *Cambridge Economic History of India*, Vol. II, ed. by Dharma Kumar (Cambridge, Cambridge University Press, 1982), pp. 558-9.
2. Tapan Raychaudhuri, 'Mid-Eighteenth Century Background' in ibid., pp. 34-5.
3. The following is a sample of the arguments supporting the view that preconditions for industrial transition could have developed without the colonial intervention. 'I am not suggesting the regions in question [Gujarat and Bengal] were quivering [in the seventeenth and eighteenth centuries] on the brink of industrialisation—a noble prospect that was foiled by colonial exploitation. It is my very limited hypothesis that the conditions in these regions were favourable rather than unfavourable to industrialisation and a different set of historical accidents, e.g. failure of the East India Company to occupy these territories and a decision of the local powers to modernize the army in order to resist Western aggressions might have led to different pattern of economic change . . . from Indian armies commanded by European generals to Indian armament factories run by Western experts might not have been a very long step.' T. Raychaudhuri, 'A Reinterpretation of Nineteenth Century Indian Economic History?' *Indian Economic and Social History Review*, Vol. 5, No. 1 (March 1968), p. 87. The feeble and defensive tone of the argument is self-revealing and needs no elaboration. Raychaudhuri, however, seems to have changed his position later as the following quotation indicates:

   > India lacked many of the positive tendencies evident in the economy of contemporary Japan. . . . For one thing, the trunk roads of the Mughals, usable only part of the year, were not comparable to the transport network of Tokugawa Japan. The Japanese merchant did not have to cope with internal tool barriers. Two-way trade between town and country was an established fact of Japanese life already in the seventeenth century. Technological progress, helped by a high level of literacy, was a feature of Tokugawa agriculture which had a firmly established rate of growth long before the Meiji restoration. And, insofar as intangibles are relevant, the Japanese elite in the seventeenth century evinced an active—and for them, dangerous—curiosity about Western science and technology which had no equivalent in contemporary India. Again, all these do not add up to a possibility of spontaneous industrialization. Pre-Meiji Japan was not moving in this direction more than

Mughal India was. Only her society and economy more than those of pre-colonial India had the potentiality to respond to opportunity positively. (Raychaudhuri, 'Mid-Eighteenth Century Background . . . ', pp. 33-5.)

4. For detailed discussion see Lakshmi Subramanian and Rajat Ray 'Merchants and Politics: From the Great Mughals to the East India Company' in *Business and Politics in India: A Historical Perspective*, ed. by Dwijendra Tripathi (New Delhi: Manohar, 1991), pp. 19-85; A.R. Kulkarni, 'Indian Business and the Marathas', V.K. Bawa, 'Business and the Princely States: The Case of Mysore' and Dwijendra Tripathi, 'Business and the Princely States: The Case of Baroda' in *State and Business in India: A Historical Perspective*, ed. by Dwijendra Tripathi (New Delhi, Manohar, 1986); John Hurd II, 'The Influence of British Policy on Industrial Development in the Princely State of India, 1890-1933', *Indian Economic and Social History Review*, Vol. XII, No. 4 (Oct-Dec. 1975). Raman Mahadevan, 'Some Aspects of Industrial Investment and Entrepreneurship in Travancore during the 1930s and 1940s presented at seminar on 'South Indian Economy, *c.* 1914-*c.* 1945' at Centre for Development Studies, Trivandrum, 25-7 April 1988.
5. David Thorner, no friend of imperialism or colonialism, has conceded this point in the following words: 'Had the British never come to India, the great likelihood is not that India by now would have transformed itself into a leading economic power, but rather that there would have been an even slighter degree of industrialisation . . .', 'The Pattern of Railway Development in India' in his *Shaping of Modern India* (New Delhi: Modern Publishers, 1980), p. 124. Long ago, Karl Marx had pointed to the role of British colonialisms in generating a 'social revolution' without which no progress, according to him was possible. K Marx and F. Engels. *The First Indian War of Independence, 1857-1859* (Moscow: Progress Publishers, 1959), p. 20.
6. Rostow in 1960 had tentatively concluded that India had 'launched' its take off around 1952, but it was too early to judge whether the launch would be successful. W.W. Rostow, *Stages of Economic Growth* (Combridge: Cambridge University Press, 1960), pp. 9, 38. There has been no systematic study since then whether the country actually attained the take off and if so when. Most observers, however, believe that the initiatives of the early 50s could not be sustained subsequently. Raj Krishna's phrase the 'Hindu Rate of Growth' with his intended pejorative connotation sums up the general consensus about the post-independence pace of Indian economic progress. My discussions with J.L. Sandesara, Dinesh Awasthi and Pradeep Keshari

have helped me clarify this point. For a comprehensive and competent discussion see Isher J. Ahluwalia, *Productivity and Growth in Indian Manufacturing* (New Delhi: Oxford University Press, 1991).

7. Western models of economic development can be identified either with capitalism or socialism. The socialist antipathy of private enterprise, which the latter reciprocated in full measure, needs no elaboration. But even the capitalist doctrines fuelled distrust between the government and business. The industrial policy pursued by the successive governments of free India, falling somewhere between the two, did even more so Whether the recent move towards economic liberalisation would reverse the process is yet to be seen.

Bibliography

Abul Fazl, *Ain-i-Akbari*, tr. by H. Blockman (Delhi: Oriental Books Reprint Corporation, 1977), Vol. 1.

Adam, Don, *Education and Modernization in Asia* (Reading, Mass: Addison-Wesley Publishing Co., 1970).

Ahluwalia, Isher J., *Productivity and Growth in Indian Manufacturing* (New Delhi: Oxford University Press, 1991).

Allen, G.C., *A Short Economic History of Modern Japan* (London: George Allen and Unwin, 1968).

Ambirajan, S., 'Changing Attitudes Towards Business in India' in *Business and Politics in India: A Historical Perspective*, ed. by Dwijendra Tripathi (New Delhi: Manohar, 1991).

Andrew Yule & Co., *Andrew Yule and Company Limited, 1863-1963* (Calcutta: Andrew Yule & Co., 1963).

Anstey, Vera, *Economic Development of India* (London: Longman's Green & Co., 1924).

Antrobus, H.A., *The History of the Assam Company, 1853-1953* (Edinburgh: Assam Co., 1957).

Arasarathnam, S., 'Indian Merchants and Their Trading Methods—*Circa* 1700', *Indian Economic and Social History Review*, Vol. 3, No. 1 (March 1966).

———, 'India and Indian Ocean: The Seventeenth Century' in *India and the Indian Ocean 1599-1800*, ed. by Ashin Das Gupta and M.N. Pearson (Calcutta: Oxford University Press, 1987).

Badshah, Bhagwanlal R., *Rao Bahadur Ranchhodlal Chhotalal C.I.E.* (Ahmedabad: Aryodaya Press, 1899).

Bagchi, A.K., *Private Investment in India, 1900-1939* (Cambridge: Combridge University Press, 1972).

Balkrishna, *Commercial Relations between India and England* (Oxford: Oxford University Press, 1924).

Banarasidas, *Ardhakathanak* (Half a Tale), ed. by Nathuram Premi (Bombay: Sanshodhita Sahityamala, 1957).

Banerjee, Tarashakar, *Internal Market of India, 1934-1900* (Calcutta: Academic Publishers, 1966).

Barber, Bernard, 'Social Mobility in Hindu India' in *Social Mobility in the Caste System in India* (The Hague: Mouton Publishers, 1968).

Basu, S.K., *The Managing Agency System* (Calcutta: The World Press, 1958).

Bawa, V.K., 'Business and the Princely States: The Case of Mysore' in *State and Business in India: A Historical Perspective*, ed. by Dwijendra Tripathi (New Delhi: Manohar, 1987).

Bellah, R., *Tokugawa Religion: The Values of Industrial Japan* (New York: Free Press, 1957).

Berna, James H., *Industrial Entrepreneurship in Madras State* (Bombay: Asia Publishing House, 1960).

Bhat, V.V., *Aspects of Economic Change and Policy in India, 1800-1960* (Bombay: Allied Publishers, 1963).

Bhattacharya, S., 'Cultural and Social Constraints on Technological Innovation and Development: Some Case Studies' in *Science, Technology and Culture*, ed. by Surajit Sinha (New Delhi: India International Centre, 1970).

———, 'Laissez Faire in India', *Indian Economic and Social History Review*, Vol. 2, No. 1 (Jan. 1965).

Bhattacharya, Sukumar, *The East India Company and the Economy of Bengal, 1704-1740* (London: Luzac & Co., 1954).

Binny Limited, *The House of Binny* (Madras: Binny Ltd., 1969).

Birla, G.D., *In the Shadow of the Mahatma* (Bombay: Orient Longman, 1955).

Black, Cyril E. *et al.*, *The Modernization of Japan and Russia: A Comparative Study* (New York: Free Press, 1975).

Black, George, *B.I. Centenary, 1858-1956* (London: Collins, 1956).

Borton, Hugh, *Peasant Uprisings in Japan of the Tokugawa Period* (New York: Paragon Book Reprint Corp., 1968).

Brimmer, Andrew F., 'The Setting of Entrepreneurship in India', *Quarterly Journal of Economics*, Vol. 119, No. 4 (Nov. 1955).

Brown. H., *Parrys of Madras* (Madras: Parry & Co., 1954).

Buchanan, D.H., *The Development of Capitalistic Enterprise in India* (New York: Macmillan Co., 1934).

Cassels, Walter R., *Cotton, An Account of Its Culture in the Bombay Presidency* (Bombay: Government Press, 1862).

Chandra, Bipan, *The Rise and Growth of Economic Nationalism in India* (New Delhi: People's Publishing House, 1979).

Chaudhuri, K.N. 'Foreign Trade and Balance of Payment (1757-1947)' in *Cambridge Economic History of India, Vol. II, c. 1757-c. 1970*, ed. by Dharma Kumar (Cambridge: Cambridge University Press, 1982).

———, 'Markets and Traders in India during the Seventeenth and Eighteenth Century' in *Economy and Society: Essays in Indian Economic and Social History*, ed. by K.N. Chaudhuri and Clive J.

Dewey (Delhi: Oxford University Press, 1979).

Chaudhari, Susil, *Trade and Commercial Organization in Bengal, 1650-1720* (Calcutta: Firma K.L. Mukhopadhyay, 1975).

Cole, Arthur H., 'An Approach to the Study of Entrepreneurship', *Journal of Economic History*, Vol. 6, Supplement (1946).

———, *Business Enterprise in its Social Setting* (Cambridge: Harvard University Press, 1959).

Dasgupta, A., *Indian Merchants and the Decline of Surat c. 1700-1750* (Wiesbaden: Franz Steiner Verlag, 1979).

———, 'The Merchants of Surat, *c.* 1700-50' in *Elites in South Asia*, ed. by E. Leach and S.N. Mukherjee (Combridge: Cambridge University Press, 1970).

Desai, Ashok V., 'The Origins of Parsi Enterprise', *Indian Economic and Social History Review*, Vol. 5, No. 4 (Dec. 1968).

Dhar, P.N. and Omkar Seth, 'The Rate of Technical Progress in the Tata Iron and Steel Company in 1913-56', *Indian Economic Review*, Vol. 16, No. 1 (Feb. 1962).

Devra, G.S.L., 'The Mughal State and Indian Business' in *State and Business in India: A Historical Perspective*, ed. by Dwijendra Tripathi (New Delhi: Manohar, 1987).

Divekar, V.D., 'The Emergence of an Indigenous Business Class in Maharashtra in the Eighteenth Century', *Modern Asian Studies* Vol. 16, No. 3 (Oct. 1982).

Dor, Ronald P., *Education in Tokugawa Japan* (London: Routledge & Kegan Paul, 1965).

Earl, David N., *Emperor and Nation in Japan* (Seattle: University of Washington Press, 1964).

Edwardes, S.M., *Memoir of Rao Bahadur Ranchhodlal Chhotalal C.I.E.* (Exter: William Pollard & Co., 1920).

Fox, Richard G., *Lions of the Punjab: Culture in the Making* (Berkeley: University of California Press, 1985).

Fukuzawa H., 'Cotton Mill Industry' in *Economic History of India*, ed. by V.B. Singh (Bombay: Allied Publishers, 1965).

Furell, James W., *The Tagore Family: Memoir* (Calcutta: T.C. Bose & Co., 1870).

Gadgil, D.R., *Origins of Modern Indian Business Class* (New York: Institute of Pacific Relations, 1959).

Galowin, Captain Vasilii, *Memoirs of Captivity in Japan* (London: Henry C. Colburn Cos., 1824).

Gerschenkron, Alexander, *Continuity in History and Other Essays* (Cambridge: Harvard University Press, 1968).

———, *Economic Backwardness in Historical Perspective* (Cambridge: Mass., Belknap Press, 1962).

———, 'Economic Backwardness in Historical Perspective' in *Progress of Underdeveloped Area*, ed. by Bert F. Hoslittz (Chicago: Chicago University Press, 1952).

Gokhale, B.G., *Surat in the Seventeenth Century: A Study in Urban History of Modern India* (London: Curzon Press, 1979).

Gopal, Surendra, 'Jain Merchants in Eastern India under Great Mughals' in *Business Communities of India: A Historical Perspective*, ed. by Dwijendra Tripathi (New Delhi: Manohar, 1984).

Goswami, Omkar, 'Then Came the Marwaris: Some Aspects of the Changes in the Pattern of Industrial Control in Eastern India'. *Indian Economic and Social History Review*, Vol. 22, No. 3 (Sept. 1985).

———, 'Sahibs, Babus and Banias: Changes in Industrial Control in Eastern India, 1918-1960', presented at the Seminar on 'Strategy and Structure in Indian Business: A Historical Perspective' at Indian Institute of Management, Ahmedabad, April 1987.

Griffiths, Perceival, *The History of the Indian Tea Industry* (London: Weidenfeld & Nicholson, 1967).

Grover, C.F., *Indian Weights and Measures* (Bombay: Government Press, 1865).

Guha, Amlendu, 'Comprador Role of Parsi Sheths, 1750-1850', *Economic and Political Weekly*, Vol. 55, No. 8 (28 Nov. 1970).

———, 'More About the Parsi Sheths: Their Roots, Entrepreneurship and Comprador Role, 1650-1918' in *Business Communities of India*, ed. by Dwijendra Tripathi (New Delhi: Manohar, 1984).

Habakkuk, H.J., 'The Historical Experience on the Basic Conditions of Economic Progress', *Economic Progress*, ed. by Leon H. Dupriez (Louvain: Institute de Recherches Economiquest Sociales, 1955).

Habib, Irfan, 'Technology and Barriers to Social Change in Mughal India', *Indian Historical Review*, Vol. 5, Nos. 1-2 (July 1978-Jan. 1979).

Hagen, Everette E., *On the Theory of Social Change* (Homewood, Ill.: Dorsey Press, 1962).

Hall, J.W., *Government and Local Power in Japan, 500 to 1700* (Princeton: Princeton University Press, 1966).

———, 'The Castle Town and Japan's Modern Urbanization', *Far Eastern Quarterly*, Vol. 15, No. 1 (Nov. 1955).

Hamilton, C.J., *The Trade Relations Between England and India* (Calcutta: Thacker Spink and Co., 1919).

Harris, F.R., *Jamsetji Nusserwanji Tata: A Chronicle of His Life* (London: Blackie & Son, 1958).

Harrison, Godfrey, *Bird and Company of Calcutta* (Calcutta: Bird & Co., 1964).

Hauser, William B., *Economic Institutional Change in Tokugawa Japan* (Cambridge: Cambridge University Press, 1974).

Hazari R.K., *The Structure of the Private Corporate Sector: A Study of Concentration, Ownership and Control* (Bombay: Asia Publishing House, 1966).

Hendrick, Burton J., *The Life of Andrew Carneqie* (London: William Heinemann, 1933).

Hirashima, S., 'Growth, Equity and Labour Absorption in Japanese Agriculture' in *Labour Absorption and Growth in Agriculture: China and Japan*, ed. by Shigeru Ishikawa *et al.* (Bangkok: International Labour Organisation, 1982).

Hirschmeier, J., 'Entrepreneurs and the Social Order: America, Germany and Japan', *Social Order and Entrepreneurship*, ed. by K. Nakagawa (Tokyo: University of Tokyo Press, 1977).

———, *The Origins of Entrepreneurship in Meiji Japan* (Cambridge: Harvard University Press, 1964).

Hirschmeier, J. and T. Yui, *Development of Japanese Business, 1600-1983* (London: George Allen and Unwin, 1985).

Hurd II, John, 'The Influence of British Policy on Industrial Development in the Princely States, 1890-1933', *Indian Economic and Social History Review*, Vol. 12, No. 4 (Oct.-Dec., 1975).

International Labour Organisation, *The World Textile Industry, Economic and Social Problem* (Geneva: I.L.O., 1937).

Ishikawa, S., *Economic Development in Asian Perspective* (Tokyo: Kinokuniya, 1967).

Ito, Shoji, 'A Note on the Business Combine in India—With Special Reference to the Nattukottai Chettiers', *Developing Economies*, Vol, 4, No. 3 (Sept. 1966).

Jain, L.C., *Indigenous Banking in India* (London: Macmillan, 1929).

Jansen, Marieus B., 'Tokugawa and Modern Japan', *Studies in Institutional History of Early Modern Japan*, ed. by J.W. Hall (Princeton: Princeton University Press, 1968).

Joshi, Arun, *Lala Shri Ram: A Study in Entrepreneurship and Industrial Management* (New Delhi: Orient Longman, 1975).

Kaempfer, E., *History of Japan* (New York: A.M.S. Press, 1978, rpt.).

Kapp, K. William, *Hindu Culture, Economic Development and Economic Planning in India* (New York: Asia Publishing House, 1963).

Kawasaki, Ichiro, *The Japanese Are Like That* (Rulland, Vt.:, C.E. Tuttle, 1955).

Khan, S.A., *The East India Trade in the Seventeenth Century in Political and Economic Aspects* (Oxford: Oxford University Press, 1923).

Kiyokawa, Yukihiko, 'Entrepreneurship and Innovations in Japan: An Application of the Experience of Technological Development in the Textile Industry', *Developing Economies*, Vol. 27, No. 3 (Sept. 1984).

———, 'Technical Adaptation and Managerial Resources in India: A Study of the Experience of the Cotton Textile Industry from a Comparative Viewpoint', *Developing Economies*, Vol. 21, No. 2 (June 1983).

———, 'Transplantation of the European Factory System and Adaptations in Japan: The Experience of the Tomioka Model Filature' (Discussion Paper No. 98, Institute of Economic Research, Hitotsubashi University, 1984).

Kling, Blair B., *Partner in Empire: Dwarkanath Tagore and the Age of Enterprise in Eastern India* (Berkeley: University of California Press, 1976).

———, 'The origin of the Managing Agency System in India', *Journal of Asian Studies*, Vol. 26, No. 1 (Nov. 1966).

Knowles. L.C.A., *The Economic Development of British Overseas Empire* (London: George & Routledge, 1928).

Kobayashi, K. and M. Kobayashi, 'Government Promotion of Manufacturing as a Precondition for Industrialization' in *Government and Business*, ed. by K. Nakagawa (Tokyo: University of Tokyo Press, 1980).

Kochanek, Stanley, *Business and Politics in India* (Berkeley: University of California Press, 1974).

Kopf, David, *The Brahmo Samaj and the Shaping of the Modern Indian Mind* (Princetion: Princeton University Press, 1970).

Kulkarni, A.R., 'Indian Business and the Marathas' in *State and Business in India: A Historical Perspective*, ed. by Dwijendra Tripathi (New Delhi: Manohar, 1984).

Kunio, Yushihara, *Sogo Shosha: The Vanguard of the Japanese Economy* (Tokyo: Oxford University Press, 1982).

Kuznets, Simon, *et al.* (ed.), *Economic Growth: Brazil, India, Japan* (Durham: Duke University Press, 1955).

Kuznets, S., *Modern Economic Growth: Rate, Structure and Spread* (New Haven: Yale University Press, 1966).

Lehman, Jean-Pierre, *The Roots of Modern Japan* (London: Macmillan Press, 1982.

Little, J.H., *The House of Jagat Seth* (Calcutta: Calcutta Historical Society, 1967).

Loknathan, P.S., *Industrial Organization in India* (London: George Allen & Unwin, 1935).

Mahadevan, Raman, 'Entrepreneurship and Business Communities in Colonial Madras, 1900-1929' in *Business Communities of India: A Historical Perspective*, ed. by Dwijendra Tripathi (New Delhi: Manohar, 1984).

———, 'Some Aspects of the Pattern of Industrial Investment and Entrepreneurship in Travancore during the 1930s and 1940s' presented at a seminar on 'South Indian Economy, *c.* 1914-

c. 1945 at Centre for Development Studies', Trivandrum, 25-7 April 1988.

Majumdar, R.C. *et al.* (eds.), *British Paramountcy and Indian Renaissance*, pt. II, (Bombay: Bharatiya Vidya Bhavan, 1965).

Marshall, B.K., *Capitalism and Nationalism in Pre-War Japan: The Ideology of the Business Elite* (Stanford: Standford University Press, 1967).

Masao, Maryuama, *Thought and Behaviour in Modern Japanese Politics* (Oxford: Oxford University Press, 1963).

Marx, K. and F. Engels, *The First Indian War of Independence, 1857-1859* (Moscow: Progress Publishers, 1959).

McClleland, David C., *The Achieving Society* (Princeton: Princeton University Press, 1961).

Medhora, P.B., 'Entrepreneurship in India', *Political Science Quarterly*, Vol. 80, No. 4 (Dec. 1965).

Mehta, S.D., *Cotton Mills of India 1854-1954* (Bombay: Textile Association, 1954).

Mitra, Kissory Chand, *Memoir of Dwarkanath Tagore* (Calcutta: Thacker Spink & Co., 1870).

Moreland, W.H., *India from Akbar to Aurangzeb* (London: Macmillan & Co., 1923).

Morishima, M., *The Economic Theory of Modern Society* (Cambridge: The University Press, 1976).

Morris, Morris D., 'Towards a Reinterpretation of the 19th Century Indian Economic History', *Journal of Economic History*, Vol. 23, No. 4 (Dec. 1963).

———, 'Values as an Obstacle to Economic Growth in South Asia: An Historical Survey', *Journal of Economic History*, Vol. 27, No. 4, Dec. 1967).

———, 'South Asian Entrepreneurship and the Rashomon Effect', *Explorations in Economic History*, Vol. 16, No. 1 (July 1979).

———, 'The Growth of Large-Scale Industry' in *Cambridge Economic History of India*, Vol. II, ed. by Dharma Kumar (Cambridge: Cambridge University Press, 1982).

Nakagawa, Keiichiro (ed.) *Social Order and Entrepreneurship* (Tokyo: Tokyo University Press, 1977).

Namboodiripad, K.N.S., *A Short History of Indian Currency* (Poona: Continental Prakashan, 1955).

Nevins, Allan, *Study in Power: John D. Rockefeller, Industrialist and Philanthropist* (New York: Charles Scribners & Sons, 1953).

Nigam, Raj K., *Managing Agencies in India* (New Delhi: Govt. of India Publication Division, 1957).

Okhawa, Kazushi and G. Ranis (eds.), *Japan and the Developing Countries: A Comparative Analysis* (New York: Basil Blackwell, 1985).

Okhawa, K. and H. Rosovsky, 'A Century of Japanese Economic Growth' in *The State and Economic Enterprise in Japan*, ed. by W.W. Lockwood (Princeton: Princeton University Press, 1965).

O'Malley, L.S.S., *Modern India and the West* (Oxford: Oxford University Press, 1925).

Ono, Akiro, 'Borrowed Technology in Iron & Steel: Brazil, India and Japan' in *Japan and the Developing Countries*, ed. by K. Okhawa and G. Ranis (New York: Basil Blackwell, 1985).

Otsuka K., G. Ranis, and G. Saxonhouse, *Comparative Technology Choice in Development: The Indian and Japanese Cotton Textile Industries* (New York: St. Martin's Press, 1988).

Pandit, D.P., 'Creative Response in Indian Economy: A Regional Analysis', *Economic Weekly*, Vol. 9, No. 9 (2 March 1957).

Pant, D., *The Commercial Policy of the Mughalas* (Bombay: D.B. Tarporawala & Sons, 1930).

Parikh, N.N., *Directory of Ahmedabad Mill Industry, 1929-1955* (Ahmedabad: N.N. Parikh, 1958).

Philips, C.H., *The East India Company, 1784-1834* (Bombay: Oxford University Press, 1961).

Piramal, Gita and Margaret Herdeek, *India's Industrialists*, Vol. 1 (Washington, D.C.: Three Continents Press, 1985).

Prakash, Om, *The Dutch East India Company and the Economy of Bengal, 1630-1720* (Delhi: Oxford University Press, 1988).

———, 'On Coinage in Mughal India', *Indian Economic and Social History Review*, Vol. 25, No. 4 (Dec. 1988).

Rahman, A. *Intellectual Colonization: Science and Technology in East-West Relations* (New Delhi: Vikas, 1983).

Rahman A. *et al.*, *Science and Technology in India* (New Delhi: Indian Council for Cultural Relations, 1973).

Ranis, G., 'The Community Centred Entrepreneur in Japanese Development', *Explorations in Entrepreneurial History*, Vol. 8, No. 2 (April 1955).

Ranis, Gustav and Gary Saxonhouse, 'Determinants of Technology Choice: The Indian and Japanese Cotton Industries' in *Japan and Developing Countries: A comparative Analysis*, ed. by K. Okhawa and Gustav Ranis (New York, Basil Blackwell, 1985).

Rawat, P.L., *History of Indian Education* (Agra: Ram Prasad & Sons, 1968).

Ray, Rajat K., *Industrialization in India* (New Delhi: Oxford University Press, 1979).

Raychaudhuri, T., 'A Reinterpretation of Nineteenth Century Indian Economic History', *Indian Economic and Social History Review*, Vol. 5, No. 1 (March 1968).

———, 'The Mid-Eighteenth Century Background' in *The Cambridge*

Economic History of India, Vol. II, ed. by Dharma Kumar (Cambridge: Cambridge University Press, 1982).

———, 'The Mughal Empire' in *The Cambridge Economic History of India* Vol. I, ed. by T. Raychaudhary and Irfan Habib (Cambridge: Cambridge University Press, 1978).

Roberts, John C., *Mitsui* (New York: Waterhill, 1973).

Rogues, George, 'Of Trade and Traders in 17th Century India', trans. and ed. by Indrani Ray, Occasional Paper No. 26 (Calcutta: Centre for Studies in Social Sciences 1979, Mimeo).

Rostow, W.W., *Stages of Economic Growth* (Cambridge: Cambridge University Press, 1960).

Rungta, Radhey Shyam, *Rise of Business Corporations in India, 1850-1900* (Cambridge: University Press, 1970).

Russell, Olando D., *The House of Mitsui* (Westport: Greenwood Press, 1939).

Rutnagur, S.S. (ed.), *Bombay Industries: The Cotton Mills* (Bombay: Bombay Textile Journal, 1927).

Sadler, Arthur L., *The Maker of Modern Japan: The Life of Tokugawa Ieyasu, 1542-1616* (London: George Allen and Unwin, 1937).

Sansom, George B., *The Western World and Japan* (New York: Knopf, 1951).

Sarkar, Jadunath, *Lectures on Mughal Administration* (Calcutta: M.C. Sarkar & Sons Pvt. Ltd., 1921).

Sarkar, Sumit, *Modern India, 1885-1947* (New Delhi: Macmillan, 1985).

Saxonhouse, Gary, 'Technology Choice in Cotton Textile Manufacturing' in *Japan and Developing Countries: A Comparative Analysis*, ed. by K. Okhawa & G. Ranis (New York, Basil Blackwell, 1985).

Say, Jean B., *Catechism of Political Economy* (London: Sherwood, 1816).

———, *A Treatise on Political Economy* (New York: A.M. Kelley, 1964, first published in French in 1803).

Sayigh, Yusif A., *Entrepreneurs of Lebanon* (Cambridge: Harvard University Press, 1962).

Schmoller, Gustav, 'The Historical Development of the Enterprise' in *Enterprise and Secular Change,* a collection of articles written during 1880-93 and edited by Frederick C. Lane (Homewood, Ill, Irwin, 1953).

Schumpeter, Joseph A., 'Creative Response in Economic History', *Journal of Economic History*, Vol. 7, No. 2 (Nov. 1947).

———, *Theory of Economic Development* (Cambridge: Harvard Universisty Press, 1934).

Seki, Keize, *The Cotton Industry of Japan* (Tokyo: Japan Society for the Promotion of Science, 1956).

Shelden, C.P., *The Rice of Merchant Class in Tokugawa Japan, 1600-1866* (New York: Russell & Russel, 1958).

Siddiqi, Asiya, 'The Business World of Jamsetjee Jejeebhoy', *Indian Economic and Social History Review*, Vol. 19, Nos. 3 and 4 (July and Dec. 1982).

Singh, S.B., *European Agency Houses in Bengal* (Calcutta: Firma K.L. Mukhopadhyaya & Co., 1966).

Sinha, N.K., 'Indian Business Enterprises: Its Failure in Calcutta (1800-1848)', *Bengal—Past and Present*, Diamond Jubilee Number (July-Dec. 1967).

———, 'Sources and Problems of Business History in India in the First Half of the 19th Century', *Proceedings of the 37th Session* (New Delhi: Indian Historical Records Commission, 1966).

Smith, Thomas C., 'Landlords and Rural Capitalists in the Modernization of Japan', *Journal of Political Economy*, Vol. 14, No. 2 (1956).

———, 'Okura Nagatsune and the Technologists' in *Personality in Japanese History*, ed. by Albert M. Craig and D.H. Shively (Berkeley: University of California Press, 1970).

———, *The Agrarian Origins of Modern Japan* (Stanford: Stanford University Press, 1959).

———, 'The Land Tax in the Tokugawa Period', *Journal of Asian Studies*, Vol. 18, No. 1 (Nov. 1958).

Spodek, Howard, 'Manchesterization of Ahmedabad', *Economic Weekly*, Vol. 17, No. 11 (13 March 1965).

Storry, G.R., *The Way of the Samurai* (London: Orbis, 1978).

Subramanian Lakshmi and Rajat K. Ray, 'Merchants and Politics: From the Great Mughals to the East India Company' in *Business and Politics in India: A Historical Perspective*, ed. by Dwijendra Tripathi (New Delhi: Manohar, 1991).

Subramanian, Sanjay and C.A. Bayly, 'Portfolio Capitalists and the Political Economy of Early Modern India', *Indian Economic and Social History Review*, Vol. 25, No. 4 (Oct.-Dec. 1988).

Takahashi, Kamekichi, *The Rise and Development of Japan's Modern Economy* (Tokyo: The Jiji Press, 1969).

Takekoshi, Yosoburo, *The Economic Aspects of the History and the Civilization of Japan* (London: Dawson of Pall Mall, 1967).

Tara Chand, *Society and the State in the Mughal Period* (New Delhi: Government of India Publications Division, 1961).

Tata Iron and Steel Co., *Tata Steel Diamond Jubilee, 1907-67* (Jamshedpur: TISCO, 1967).

Teratani, Takeaki, 'Japanese Business and Government in the Take off Stage' in *Government and Business*, ed. by K. Nakagawa (Tokyo: University of Tokyo Press, 1980).

Textile Institute, *Mangement in the Textile Industry* (Manchester: Textile Institute, 1969).

Thomas K.P., 'The History of the House of Martin Burn', *Homma's Annual of Calcutta* (Calcutta: K.P. Thomas, 1953).

Thorner, D., *Land and Labour in India* (Bombay: Asia Publishing House, 1962).

———, *The Shaping of Modern India* (New Delhi: Allied Publishers, 1980).

Timberg, Thomas A., *The Marwaris from Traders to Industrialists* (New Delhi: Vikas, 1980).

Tirmizi, S.A.I., 'Muslim Merchants of Medieval Gujarat', in *Business Communities of India: A Historical Perspective*, ed. by Dwijendra Tripathi (New Delhi: Manohar, 1984).

Tripathi, Dwijendra 'Birth, Growth and Death of Firms in a Proto-Industrial Economy: The Experience of the Ahmedabad Textile Industry, 1858-1929, *Indian Historical Review*, Vol. 16, Nos. 1-2 (July 1989 and Jan. 1990).

———, 'Colonialism and Technology Choices in India: A Historical Overview', *Developing Economies*, Vol. 34, No. 1 (March 1996).

———, 'Congress and the Indian Industrialists, 1885-1947' in *Business and Politics in India: A Historical Perspective*, ed. by Dwijendra Tripathi (New Delhi: Manohar, 1991).

———, 'From Community to Class: Marwaris in Historical Perspective' in *Economic Times* (Calcutta) *Marwaris of Calcutta*, Special Feature (30 April 1988).

———, 'Opportunism of Free Trade: Lancashire Cotton Famine and Indian Cotton Cultivation', *Indian Economic and Social History Review*, Vol. 4, No. 3 (Sept. 1967).

———, 'Opportunism of Free Trade: Sadasheogarh Harbour Project, 1855-1865 , *Indian Economic and Social History Review*, Vol. 5, No. 4 (Dec. 1968).

———, *The Dynamics of a Tradition: Kasturbhai Lalbhai and His Entrepreneurship* (New Delhi: Manohar, 1981).

———, 'The Silver Question: India and America', *Journal of Indian History*, Vol. 44, No. 132 (Sept. 1967).

———, 'An Echo Beyond the Horizon: The Effect of the American Civil War on India', *Journal of Indian History*, Golden Jubilee Volume (Trivandrum: University of Kerala, 1973).

———, 'An Integrated View of Entrepreneurship', in *Economic and Political Weekly*, Vol. 20, No. 48 (30 Nov. 1985).

———, 'Business and the Princely States: The Case of Baroda' in *State and Business in India: A Historical Perspective*, ed. by Dwijendra Tripathi (New Delhi: Manohar, 1984).

———, 'Innovations in Indian Textile Industry: The Formative Years' in *Textile Industry and Its Business Climate*, ed. by A. Okochi and

S. Yonekawa (Tokyo: University of Tokyo Press, 1982).

———, 'Occupational Mobility and Industrial Entrepreneurship in India: A Historical Survey', *Developing Economics*, Vol. 19, No. 1 (March 1981).

———, 'The United States and India: Economic Links 1860-1900', Ph.D. Dissertation (University of Wisconsin, Madison, 1963).

Tripathi, Dwijendra and M.J. Mehta, 'Class Character of the Gujarati Business Community' in *Business Communities of India: A Historical Perspective*, ed. by Dwijendra Tripathi (New Delhi: Manohar, 1984).

———, *Business Houses in Western India: A Study In Entrepreneurial Response 1850-1956* (New Delhi: Manohar, 1990).

Tripathi, Dwijendra and Priti Misra, *Towards a New Frontier: History of the Bank of Baroda* (New Delhi: Manohar, 1985).

Tsukahira, T.G., *Feudal Control in Tokugawa Japan: The Sankinkotai System* (New York: Alfred A. Knopf, 1969).

Tsunoda, Ryusaku *et al.* (eds.), *Sources of Japanese Tradition* (New York: Columbia Press, 1965).

Tsurumi, Yoshi, *Japanese Business* (New York: Praeger Publishers, 1978).

Vakhatchand, Maganlal, *Amdavadno Itihas* in Gujarati (Ahmedabad: Gujarat Samachar, 1978 rpt).

Venkatasubbiah, H., *Enterprise and Economic Change: 50 Years of FICCI* (New Delhi: Vikas, 1977).

Verrier, Elwin, *The Story of Tata Steel* (Bombay: Tata Sons Ltd., 1958).

Wadia, R.A., *A Foregotten Friend of India: Sir Charles Forbes* (Baroda: Padmaja Publications, 1948).

Wallace, D.R., *The Romance of Jute: A Short History of the Calcutta Jute Mill Industry, 1855-1927* (London: W. Thacker, 1928).

Webb, H., *Japanese Imperial Institution in the Tokugawa Period* (New York: Columbia University Press, 1968).

Weber, Max, *Religion of India: The Sociology of Hinduism and Buddhism*, ed. by H.H. Gerth and D. Martindale (Glenco, Ill.: Free Press, 1958).

Yamamura, Kozo, *A Study of Samurai Income and Entrepreneurship* (Cambridge: Harvard University Press, 1974).

Yonekawa, Shinichi, 'Recent Writing on Japanese Economic and Social History', *Economic History Review*, Second Series, Vol. 38, No. 1 (Feb. 1935).

———, 'University Graduates in Japanese Enterprises Before the Second World War', *Business History*, Vol. 24, No. 3 (July 1984).

Index